R U Ready 4 Y?

R U Ready 4 Y?

The Business Leader's Guide
to an Emergent Generation of
Millennials in the Workforce

Lubaina Galely
Anthony Horton
Whitney Wrona

Library of Congress Control Number:		2015912922
ISBN:	Hardcover	978-1-5035-9332-9
	Softcover	978-1-5035-9331-2
	eBook	978-1-5035-9330-5

Print information available on the last page.

Rev. date: 08/17/2015

To order additional copies of this book, contact:
Xlibris
1-888-795-4274
www.Xlibris.com
Orders@Xlibris.com
715854

Contents

Intro: R U Ready?

This book is an essential read for any business leader, manager or HR professional, seeking to understand the growing differences between generations in the workplace. It is predicted that by 2025 over 70% of the workforce in North America will consist of employees from the Millennial generation. The risks to businesses that do not prepare themselves for this reality is significant as organizations compete to attract and retain talent.

There are hundreds of publications and articles on the subject of Generation Y. Many of these are focused on describing the unique mindsets and expectations within the next generation of workers. This book is different. *R U Ready 4 Y?* provides the required thought leadership and key insights on how to *practically manage and lead* this emerging generation of employees. It is intended to be thought-provoking for present day leaders and managers as well as for Millennials themselves insofar as they can evaluate how they are generally perceived by other generations in the business world. The key concepts will help with planning and strategizing for employee engagement over the coming decade.

Much of the current dialogue around Generation Y focuses on future impacts to the workplace and employee engagement. The principal basis of this guide is rooted in the assertion that the majority of leadership and managerial positions in North America and globally are currently held by individuals that come from the Boomer and Generation X cohorts. This book is of considerable value to these leaders as it outlines the prerequisite tactics to address the engagement needs and dynamics of the impending wave of employees entering the labor pool. Admittedly, much of the advice within this guide will make the average above thirty-five year old business manager mildly unnerved. Even the title, deliberately written in modern "textese", is meant to be somewhat provocative to business leaders in the Boomer and Gen X category. If you are in one of these generations, ask yourself if the unconventional title did strike you as slightly out-of-place or even improper?

Those in Gen Y itself will also find this guide of value. It will furnish the Millennial reader with awareness of the differences in thinking that they will encounter as they grow their careers. Perceptiveness to the older generations in the workplace is of great utility. It will also reaffirm for Gen Y that they are intrinsically improving the business world. Their approaches to work, open-mindedness, respect for diversity and commitment to education are truly progressive.

The authors have been deliberate in referring to this emergence as a future generational struggle. The values, expectations, viewpoints and experiences between the generations are incredibly different and often in conflict. The struggle and solution, particularly for large, established corporations - with history and entrenched foundational processes for recruitment, performance management, work structure, service, talent development and rewards and recognition - will not be easy. Failing to make dramatic changes to understand and adapt to the demands of Generation Y will have material impacts to the bottom line.

As Tara Wolckenhauer, DVP of Human Resources for Human Capital Management leader ADP points out, it is not enough to make minor adjustments in preparation for Gen Y in the workplace; it calls out for a strategy that recognizes future impacts on the full continuum of the business:

"With the incredible influx of Gen Y employees entering the workforce over the next several years, it is crucial that companies prepare and ready themselves for transformational changes. These changes will encompass all elements of the business paradigm: recruiting, tenure, total rewards, engagement, recognition, customer service and even our corporate brands."

When discussing Gen Y in the workplace, it is interesting to note that the preceding generations tend to discuss work behaviors in negative terms – often accompanied by a roll-of-the-eyes and commentary on how difficult Millennials can be to manage. It is time to move from criticism of the divergent aspects of the collective Gen Y character and start preparing to welcome this cohort of talented employees with open arms and a fresh set of eyes.

Business leaders need to first understand the sources of this conflict and then develop a broad and methodical approach to act in response.

- ✓ Those that *do* will flourish.
- X Those that *do not* risk an alienated employee base, degraded productivity and increased expense associated with a high rate of attrition.

The observations within this book will help demystify the generational gaps. It will illustrate the unique perspectives and expectations of Generation Y and outline the differences between the primary future participants in the workplace and the present-day members – the Ys and the Boomer/Gen Xs. Through fictional character-based examples, real life experiences and solutions to prepare, the reader will gain key insights and tools to attract, engage and retain tomorrow's employees.

And, the authors offer something new. Beyond the known factors that drive engagement for Generation Y, this guide culminates in a proposal: a recommendation for a new approach in the future mind-shift toward adoption of team self-management. It is a proposition drawn from the carefully illustrated strategies to address the unique motivations of Millennials. And it requires a drastic change in mindset that will also, at first, likely make some of today's Baby Boomer and Generation X business leaders uncomfortable.

It needs to be noted that the Millennial challenges we describe within this book are not a singular event in the history of modern commerce and corporations. For those leaders that are banking on things reversing or normalizing after this unique breed of employees pass through their lifecycle in the business environment, it is time to face reality. There will be no normalization or going back. The generation behind Gen Y is an amplified version of the Millennials.

1.

"These Leaders sometimes don't have a clue. There is so much I could be doing to help our company advance. But sometimes it's like no one wants to listen to my ideas. I mean, my Vice President told me he has never even sent or even read a Tweet. How out of touch is that!?"

24 year-old new employee
Generation Y

Drawing the Battle Lines: From Boomers to Millennials

As the generations collide with each other in today's – and increasingly tomorrow's – workplace, the key to success will be to understand each of the various motivating characteristics and values that compete for attention. These ultimately form the fundamental models for each generation's work behavior, expectations and their interactions. In examining these traits, it is important to "keep our eye on the ball", so to speak, and accept that the size of the Millennial age group means that they will soon overshadow all others in the labor force. Understanding their attitudes towards work and commerce is paramount as the Ys will *own the workplace* in a decade.

An examination of U.S Census Bureau data and multiple economic forecasts shows just how sizable the shifts in generational representation will be. Today, Gen Y is just barely in the dominant position:

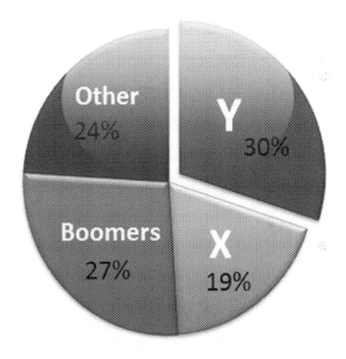

By 2025, Millennials will be the dominant influence in the workforce; they will essentially represent the preponderance of the entire labor pool (and interestingly, the number of females will tower above the number of males):

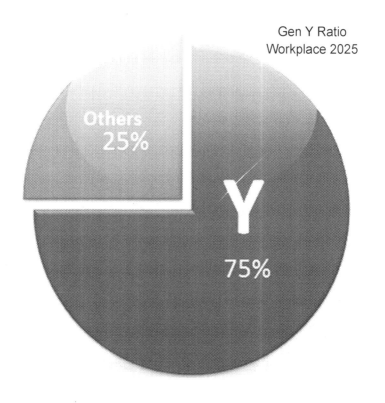

Gen Y Ratio
Workplace 2025

Others
25%

Y
75%

Gender Distribution
2025

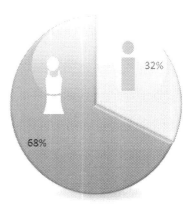

32%

68%

Consequently, the post-2020 decade will see specific changes in the workforce mix and challenges related to integrating Gen Y *en masse* into the workforce:

"Slower population growth will lead to a decreasing rate of growth in the overall labor force from 2010 to 2020: only 0.7% annually, compared with 0.8% for 2000 to 2010 and with 1.3% for 1990-2000. Within this time frame, the Baby Boom generation will shift entirely into the 55-years-and-older age group. Though the 55-plus age group will increase within the labor market, the BLS projects the 'prime-age' working group (ages 25 to 54) to drop to 63.7% of the workforce by 2020. The BLS also forecasts that there will be 54.8 million total job openings in the 2010-2020 time period with well over half - 61.6% - from 'replacement needs.'"

U.S. Bureau of Labor Statistics' (BLS) Employment Outlook: 2010-2020" report - Monthly Labor Review January 2012

This jaw-dropping number of replacement needs referenced above will be filled almost entirely from the ranks of Gen Y.

To attract and retain talent, organizational policies and work structures will have to be designed in a way that takes into account the reality of conflicting generational cultures, principles and ideologies – specifically between Boomers/Gen X and Gen Y. As much as it may be difficult for today's Boomer or Gen X leaders to accede, the changes made will need to be heavily tailored towards adaptation to Gen Y needs.

The ensuing impacts of this are so transformational that they will touch every part of the business value chain, including some that may not initially be that self-evident. For example, in 2012 Colliers published a white paper addressing the impacts that Gen Y will have on office space. It seems like such a minor thing at first glance, does it not? Here is what they predict:

"As of 2030 the Baby Boomers will be virtually non-existent in the workforce – bar any dramatic changes to the retirement age – leaving Generation Y...to dominate the workforce, buoyed by the Generation which comes next. Generation X will form one quarter of the workforce at this point in time.

We can expect a major change in the dominant style, motivation and methods of working and communicating within our modern workforce over the next 20 years, which will be reflected in the type of space demanded for use. This needs to be placed in the context of a shrinking workforce, reducing the overall demand for commercial office space."

"Generation Y: How Population
Will Impact Office Space Demand".
Colliers International White Paper: Issue 2 of 6
November 1, 2011

Given the truly unprecedented nature of the shifts that will occur as Gen Y quickly assumes its place in the workforce, there are many unanswered questions regarding the full ramifications. However, studying what we *do* know about Gen Y and the other generations presents opportunities that have a high probability of success. Understanding what drives the thinking and behaviors of each generation is of great consequence in preparing for the considerable adjustments that will be required. The generations that will be participating most within the labor pool have been generally categorized into the following segments:

- **Baby Boomers**: born between 1946 and 1964
- **Gen X**: born between 1965 and 1979
- **Gen Y/Millennial**: born between 1980 and 2000

Characteristics:

As opposed to providing an in-depth description of each of these generations' attributes, the authors have determined that it will be more instructive to "bring to life" their different beliefs, values and work ethics through several fictional characters who typify each segment.

Outlined below are three such character examples. These representative employees will be featured throughout the book, in order to illuminate several key concepts.

James   Baby Boomer

- His competitiveness makes him a hard-worker and he strives to achieve (if not exceed) all targets set. He is very focused on balancing his demanding career as an executive in a large company with his family obligations and a few hobbies.
- James is respectful of rank, hierarchy and experience in the workplace.
- His kids are both in university and he sometimes gets nervous about the high expense, although he has a good cushion in his personal savings.
- He is a team player that will sacrifice personally to climb the corporate ladder when necessary.
- He is sometimes preoccupied with thoughts about his retirement savings and whether he will have enough money to retire comfortably at an early enough age.

Michelle   Generation X

- Michelle is pragmatic, and will not waste time with non-essential activities.
- What may appear to be a lack of respect for title, rank or tenure actually stems from her view that "you get out what you put in" in terms of effort. She judges on this basis and not on the basis of hierarchy.

- *Michelle values independence and self-reliance and respects, above all else, individuality.*
- *She is loyal to the corporation she works for, but will "change brands" for the right opportunity.*
- *To her, work-life balance means focusing on continuing education in her spare time so that she can continue to steadily advance her career and be marketable should any bumps in the road arise.*
- *She prides herself on being able to manage all of this and, while she routinely puts in a solid fifty-hour work week, she consistently makes time to devote to her two teenage daughters.*

Tyler   *Millennial/Gen Y*

- *His technological savvy makes him very adaptive to the ever-changing environment.*
- *Tyler has an aptitude for multi-tasking, he is accustomed to 24/7 connectivity and is constantly using his smartphone.*
- *His entrepreneurial spirit runs deep, along with a deep-rooted need to make a difference in the world.*
- *Teamwork is valued, although in a different manner than the previous generations. Goals of the team and working together towards a common objective are critical to him.*

- *Tyler expects and may even demand workplace flexibility. He expects to have a say in the daily work affairs and wants control over how he meets his responsibilities.*
- *He has a very strong social network and values time with those whom he is closest.*

A quick examination of the values and work ethics above demonstrates why the battle lines are as definitive as they are. A core area of conflict occurs, and will continue, between Gen X and Millennials. There are a limited number of employees in the workforce of tomorrow who will not fit into the X or Y categories. At present, the majority of Boomers either occupy the highest-levels of management (for example, the C-suite) or are preoccupied with retirement, as opposed to career progression: many of them are also dealing with residual debt from the 2008 economic crisis, rebuilding retirement savings and questioning how long they will need to remain actively employed. Gen X is focused on earning their stripes within the corporate environs and balancing family obligations with work. Gen Y expects to have a high social component at work and to have a say in their work settings, which clashes directly with the previous generations' views – especially in the area of individualism and respect for experience. They expect that they will have to reinvent themselves several times throughout their careers and are motivated to choose careers that interest them versus craving titles and money. This generation has a strong desire for "full-life balance" as opposed to the more Gen X "work-life balance" definition, and social conscience plays a strong role in influencing their decision-making.

Here is where the core source of potential conflict arises. Generation X and Y are ultimately starting to share the dominant space in the workplace at present and they exhibit wide disparities in attitude, outlook and approach. Gen X is the first generation of "job jumpers" largely due to the Information Age, shifts over the past three decades from manufacturing to a more tertiary economy and the common vagaries that occur with regard to peaks and valleys in the job market. They expect and are motivated by financial rewards for their efforts. They value their experience, industriousness and work effort. The average Gen X will focus on how many hours they worked, whereas Gen Y will place greater value on the outcomes of a task performed.

In North America alone, the Boomer and Gen Y cohorts are estimated to be just over 71 million in number each; Gen X pales in comparative size at roughly 40 million. This means that attention, in terms of government policies, marketing focus, pop culture, etc. has been largely directed at and catered to the two larger contingents that bookend Gen X. Boomers and Gen Y own a much larger share of everything. Consequently, there is a degree of embedded cynicism toward Boomers and Millennials interwoven with the Gen X state-of-mind as a result of being caught between two larger generations.

Conversely, Generation Y has often been regarded as the richest of all the generations preceding them. They have had access to money and have influenced their parents and other family members in decisions, from the very basic, such as which movie to go to on Friday night, to even having a say in large purchases such as the family car or home. They were, for the most part, raised by Boomers who were the first generation to have material and disposable income. Millennials have generally benefited from the vantage point of an open family wallet. This is also the first generation to leverage their parents' knowledge and experience to assist them in fundamental work choices, such as where to seek employment and which benefits are in their best interest.

Generation X was raised by older Boomers and younger parents from the generation prior to the Boomers. Generation X has been instilled with the values of self-reliance. Gen X, unlike Gen Y, was not consulted on family decisions and when they entered the workforce did not consult heavily with their parents on how to succeed in their careers, let alone where to work or what benefits to take.

Generation Y pastimes involve much more than just hanging out at the mall or watching television. Leisure activities from a very young age involve exposure to and use of advanced technology, video games, movies, visits to amusement/theme parks; these expected activities come with significant expense. As a result, they are often accused of having a sense of entitlement and a lack of structure or parameters.

There are a number of these types of prevailing opinions – largely held by some Boomers and most Gen Xers – that have helped to fuel the underlying generational conflict in the workplace. In reality, many of these are simply preconceived generalizations. Here are a few predominant ones:

- Millennials are not loyal to their employers.
- Millennials are entitled and expect too much for too little.
- Millennials are more inclined to slack off and use technology at work for social purposes.
- Millennials will not adhere to rules.

While these "myths" are predicated on some real (but very broad) dynamics within Gen Y – they have been greatly embellished. It is important to understand what the *realities* are and what the *exaggerated myths* are, so that the myths do not dictate strategy.

In order to further elucidate the main divergences between Gen X and Y, the following hypothetical example using our fictional characters has been provided:

Michelle has recently been promoted to the role of Director, at age forty-four, after having worked for the past eight years at a Fortune 500 global corporation. This is the third company she has worked for, having started out with a large consulting firm after completing her MBA and advancing as she changed roles and organizations over the years.

Michelle recently hired Tyler, who just graduated at the age of twenty-two. Michelle was initially apprehensive at his lack of experience although her firm has recently hired more and more employees directly out of university. In the past, she had the luxury of being able to bring in seasoned recruits but she is getting used to the new reality. What is emerging with her newest recruits is that they offer access to knowledge and skills on social networking and today's fast changing tools – something that marries up nicely with the changing demographics of their customers.

Tyler surprised Michelle when his father came in on Tyler's second day at work to check out his workplace and meet his manager. She could not imagine having had her parents anywhere near her work environment at the age of twenty-two – she was already standing on her own two feet by then.

"I think I would have died on the spot if my Dad had come in to check out where I worked back then," she had exclaimed to one of her personal friends.

Later, she was outright shocked when – after only two months at the company – Tyler suggested that he would be more productive if he worked at home two days a week where he could focus without distractions.

Michelle recognizes that she and her more seasoned colleagues may be dragging their feet a bit in working toward the adaptation of their policies to a new generation of employees. However, she is appalled at the attitude of this new recruit who feels comfortable enough to speak his mind at every meeting and occasionally even seems to expect to be involved in the decisions that she sees as her responsibility. Having the audacity to request home-working arrangements without having earned this entitlement through time and proven results has made her question the decision to hire Tyler.

New recruits are expected to conform to the company policies and work rules. Also, perks are expected to be earned through years of service, loyalty and knowledge, in combination with an employee's competence. Tyler, on the other hand, is focused on what he is expected to accomplish and does not seem to put a lot of stock in years of service. He also expects his knowledge and success will warrant him a raise and/or promotion in the near future.

From Tyler's perspective, the way he looks at things is simple: achieve what needs to be done without having to worry about conforming to any stringent work schedule and/or location. He feels that he will achieve better results by working in the peace and solitude of his rented studio apartment in the city. He likes to go into work a couple of days during the week, to ensure that he stays in touch with any changes and to be involved in discussions with his teammates.

The above scenario illustrates one of the prevailing dynamics of these two generations; which is profoundly different mindsets.

The key is for Michelle to recognize, accept and prepare herself as well as her company for the different approach and thinking Tyler represents. This has to be embraced in a manner that does not alienate the seasoned and experienced personnel in the business, while still harnessing the benefits that the Ys like Tyler bring – not an easy balance.

As the example highlights, Michelle, the typical Gen X, sees her young recruit's request to work from home combined with his short tenure with the company as verging on inappropriate. Tyler, the typical Gen Y, is focused on how he can be part of the team, contribute most effectively and get the job done. He probably does not even realize that Michelle sees his inputs or requests as inappropriate and he also thinks nothing of his father checking out his workplace since his family has been a central part of all his decisions since he can remember.

Who needs to be flexible and change their established mindset in this situation? The safe answer would be to say that they both have to adapt to and understand each other's perspectives. However, it is not at all accurate to assume this. In fact, if you really contemplate it, it is Michelle that must adapt. As the employee in the leadership position it is incumbent upon her to create an environment where Tyler and potentially others in his demographic are exceedingly engaged.

Those in the Boomer and Gen X demographic tend to dismiss the generational differences as minor. The folly in this assumption is that they believe the generation following them into the workforce will be similar in terms of their motivations or that they will eventually evolve to share their points of view. In some respects, examples of similarities can be found. For example, compensation is a motivating factor in all generations. To lead with the above assumption is to miss the big picture. This is the most educated generation in the history of the developed world, with the most immediacy and accessibility to knowledge ever to enter the workforce. Make no mistake, Gen Y is driven. In fact, they have a composite 63% average attendance record in university compared to a historical rate of 25% for Gen X and Boomers. This has a dramatic impact on their expectations of the companies they work for and what work itself means as a whole.

Because it is Gen X and some Boomers who will continue assuming leadership roles in the short-term, it is their accountability to arm themselves with strategies on how to manage these new entrants to the workplace. By learning the unique perspectives of the generation that will soon represent more than half the employees in the cubicles and hallways of the world's corporations, they will be able to lead effectively. Time is of the essence in this process. Organizations don't have five years to figure these new paradigms out; they must start strategizing now to be ready within at least five years. Those who simply bury their heads in the sand and attempt to enforce their conventional structures will be doomed to fail.

2.

"I just don't understand these kids; they think a university degree and half-a-brain means they're going to have my job in eighteen months. It took me over a decade of working my butt off to get where I am today."

Middle-Manager – large global
Fortune 1000 company
Generation X

Employee Engagement: Rethinking Everything

With the introduction of Gen Y in the workplace, it is imperative to realize the rapid need for organizational change and for leaders to tailor their engagement strategies to attract and retain the right talent.

In their June 2009 *HRO Today* article, "To Engage Gen Y Workers, Adopt A New Approach", Lynn Schleeter and Louise Anderson predicted accurately in stating:

"If HR and others want to tap into the creativity, innovation, and technological savvy of this generation to grow the bottom line, it is imperative to consider

new models for on-boarding - including attracting, engaging, and retaining - Gen Y employees, especially those facing a shrinking labor force due to retiring workers."

"To Engage Gen Y Workers, Adopt New Approach"
HRO Today
Schleeter/Anderson
June 9, 2009

Technology and innovation are central to this point, in fact, central to everything Gen Y. If leaders do not adapt to new philosophies around an increasing openness to the technological connectedness of Gen Y in the workplace, the results will culminate in their companies attracting and employing only the bottom-end of the talent pool. In addition, it will stifle innovation.

Should today's Boomer and Gen X business leaders just accept at face value this new requirement for a more unobstructed approach to technology? The most common response to this question, while not being apathetic, does verge on the slightly myopic. There is often within Boomers and Gen X, a sense that the scale of Gen Y's influence and the cumulative impact that they will have on industry has been exaggerated.

Consider the following:

In his 2014 *FastCompany* article on the subject, Dr. Tomas Chamorro-Premuzic evaluated MBA students whom he has taught over the past fifteen years – from Gen X to Gen Y. He notes that the typical Gen X student wanted nothing more than to graduate and join an established Fortune 500 company, whereas the Millennial students gravitate to entrepreneurship. Gen Y, rightly or wrongly, perceive the big company as stifling creativity and they place such a high value on innovation that they prefer to take the risk of going out on their own.

"In the past few years...a new favorite career choice has emerged, which eclipses any other form of traditional employment—working for themselves or launching their own business.

This is consistent with data highlighting the global rise in self-employment and startup activity. According to World Bank data, 30% of the global population may be working for themselves, and even strong economies - where job opportunities abound - are experiencing an increase in self-employment rates. Furthermore, this pattern will only be exacerbated in the near future, when more millennials leave college to enter the job market, and when those currently in employment give up working for someone else".

"Why Millennials Want To Work For Themselves",
Dr. Tomas Chamorro-Premuzic
FastCompany,
August 13, 2014

Gen Y employees were raised in an environment with constant stimulation and variety. These same dynamics need to translate into their work setting with diversity of functions and the ability to develop skills in a variety of areas.

Organizations now have to bridge the challenge of full-life balance and the connected mentality of the younger generation with the knowledge and experience of the prior generations – with Boomers and Gen X adapting their concepts and approaches to work, in order to protect the bottom-line. The economic equation for business is simple: amending tactics and attitudes will lead to attracting top talent and securing their engagement – the resultant upshot of which will be improved employee retention and longevity which directly strengthens profit margins.

There have been numerous articles and publications regarding this subject with a vast array of recommendations to address the Gen Y workforce. The authors of this guide have determined that, of the many possible approaches that can positively contribute, there are *3 key foundational areas of focus* that organizations must concentrate on if they are to be successful in rethinking everything and driving profitable engagement with this emerging generation of workers. These are:

1. Open Approach to Technology
2. Innovation Focus
3. Location and Schedule Flexibility

1. Open Approach to Technology

Technology has rewoven the social fabric. It has quickly become the driving force behind significant upheaval in the way in which we conduct business, manage our workforce and stay connected.

Technology has created the opportunity to creatively formulate work location and structure, eliminating the need for rigid policies, at-office-only work requirements and cast-in-stone schedules. The largely Boomer/ Gen X leadership and management cohort has to adapt to this as a reality. The issue is that the average Boomer or Gen X sees workplace elements like work-from-home and flexible scheduling as perks that are earned through time and performance or, at the very least, with an equivocal suspicion that they are decretive to productivity; the average Gen Y sees them as entitlements and advantageous to productivity.

If the traditional mindsets can be adjusted, consider the potentially positive impacts on efficiency through increased Gen Y engagement.

While a majority of professionals in the Boomer/ Gen X category generally consider themselves to be technically savvy and connected, they do not fully comprehend the degree to which the following generation supersedes them. Yes, it is true that the average 40-something has an iPhone or Galaxy, is familiar with a variety of apps, is on Linkedin or

Facebook and has been using the Internet since it started. However, they apply their experiential framework to that of Gen Y, and in this they fail to grasp the extent to which this generation is *truly* connected. Social networking through technology is an immediate and often preferred method of communication for Millennials. A Gen Y will only utilize the technologies and apps that work for them; there are no tutorials, intensive training or allowances for anything not being online, available and easy-to-use, 100% of the time. While the professional in his/her forties is a heavy user of technology, the Gen Y employee *lives* technology!

Exposure to technology from a very young age has cultivated their ability to grasp and master almost anything new with alacrity. This extends to Gen Y's incredible ability to navigate and solve technical items as well.

Gen Y *bonds* with their technology, which is second nature to them. They gravitate to technologies and simply want more, their appetites whet by the speed and constancies of change and perpetual advancement. In the spirit of rethinking everything, today's business leaders need to consider a different approach around this generation and how technology plays its ineffable part.

How does this translate into viable actions for leaders? A couple of recommendations include:

- Leaders should not limit access to technologies in the workplace. This is counterintuitive to conventional management thinking which usually veers toward the mindset of "if I give them access to too much, they will drain productivity by surfing all day". The inverse is true, Gen Y workers need access to all technologies in order to be at their most productive and they have an incredible ability to multi-task with numerous simultaneous applications.

- Adopt, create and enable access to social media to encourage sharing of information, learning and problem solving within the organization. The same principle applies, despite the fact that until today many Gen X leaders are reticent to open up the social media floodgates to their employees, this new generation will leverage their access to be productive.

Over the past decade, many companies have approached social media with a sense of fear. The concept of opening access to public social networks to their employees has been debated. In some instances, organizations have developed social media policies with the intention to provide employee access but curtail certain activities. While social media policies that define limits on how employees present themselves as a representative in the public domain are important to have in place, many of the early attempts at these have been too restrictive, at least from the Gen Y point of view. The efficacy of these policies is difficult to measure. In addition, companies have struggled with how to effectively harness social media for greater productivity and improved sales or customer relationships.

Much of this has left the Millennials scratching their heads. They simply do not differentiate between "being at work" or "being off work" and having access to both public and private social networks and tools. They view any restrictions to this access as detrimental to their ability to fully function during the workday.

As an example, in 2012 the Northeast Ohio Employers Research Council published in its *2012 Social Media in the Workplace Survey* some surprising results of how organizations view social media:

- **Fifty-five percent** prohibit employee use of social media during work hours on a company-issued computer.

- **Forty-three percent** prohibit employee use of social media during work hours on a company-issued mobile device.

- **Thirty-two percent** prohibit employee use of social media during work hours on a personal mobile device.

The high percentage of restraints that companies place on employee access to social media, given the changing demographics of the workplace, is alarming. Most leaders (predominantly, if not exclusively, Baby Boomers and Gen X) cited the risk of employees "goofing off on the Internet" as the primary rationale for the constraints. In the same year that the survey above was published, *Forbes* magazine published an article by Cheryl Conner entitled "Employees Really Do Waste Time at Work". The article quotes Russ Warner, CEO of Content Watch (and himself a Gen X) as stating:

"According to a recent Salary.com survey, one of the biggest culprits is surfing the Internet.

According to the survey, a majority of employees regularly spend time surfing the Internet on websites unrelated to work. Because "time is money", every hour wasted has a direct negative impact on the bottom line."

Warner goes on to take aim at the Y Generation as the most frequent perpetrators:

"The younger, more tech-savvy worker demographic appeared to be the biggest group of recreational Web surfers."

These statements tend to galvanize the Boomers and Gen Xs' perception that opening access to social media, particularly for this fledgling generation of workers, is a risky proposition.

Later in the same article, however, Warner makes an even more important point, ostensibly still referring to the younger workers:

"Respondents said the No. 1 reason for slacking at work was that they don't feel challenged enough in their job. Other reasons include, (2) they work too many hours, (3) the company doesn't give sufficient incentive to work harder, (4) they are unsatisfied with their career, and (5) they're just bored."

"Employees Really Do Waste Time at Work"
Cheryl Conner
Forbes
July 17, 2012

Is social media the cause of the perceived "slacking" or are there other factors to focus on, while taking a less risk-averse approach to social media and technology access in the workplace? The answer seems self-evident.

In fact, leading organizations that have solved this have developed their own proprietary internal and external social networks in order to harness the power of collaboration within their work environments. They leverage social media, instead of suppressing the use of it and by doing so build better experiences for employees and enhance how they connect and communicate with one another. Interestingly, a panel survey conducted by the authors in 2015 found that *over 73% of the users* of internal social networks were between 19 and 27 years of age. And within this cohort, over 91% indicated that they used the social network as a first option (over and above internal knowledge bases, training material or managers) to resolve day-to-day business issues – over 91%! Additionally, and again within this same age group, over 68% indicated that they had used public social networks at some point in the past 12 months to research a work-related subject.

Concentrating on providing challenging work, creating opportunities to innovate and committing to career development for Generation Y represent the best pathways to preventing idle time for this age bracket and improving the bottom line through employee engagement. To continue down the current path of restricted access is to ignore the pervasiveness and interconnectedness of technology in the hands of its most adept users – Gen Y.

2. Innovation Focus

It is clear that companies need to recognize and adapt to this need to innovate – but, of course, the question is, how?

Innovation does not mean every Gen Y employee needs to be on the product development team in order to boost their engagement. What it means is that leaders have to find ways to provide the freedom and, in fact, support these employees in trying new things which are not part of their regular work routine or job functions. There is an overwhelming drive within the collective Gen Y makeup to step outside of established parameters and contribute to solutions and problem solving. This is something leaders need to channel in order to engage and drive returns. Gen X has a hard time with this: giving in to the more impulsive tendencies of their younger co-workers who seek self-discovery through innovation in their work environment does not come naturally to them. Leaders in the Gen X space and HR practitioners, in general, require customized strategies to overcome their reluctance to loosen certain controls and create a culture of innovation focus.

Here are a number of strategies to consider:

- Reconsider the elements and structure of tasks/work functions and devise ways to communicate and demonstrate their value to the organization – Gen Y wants to know that they are contributing and precisely how they are benefiting the organization.

- Focus on the success factors and end results, and let employees deduce how to get there without injecting rigidity and unnecessary rules/structure. In other words, do not tell Gen Y how to attain a business objective. Rather, describe the objective, how they are expected to contribute to it and then let them loose to creatively figure out how to reach it.

- Build a relaxed and informal atmosphere with a sense of inclusiveness. Creating an environment in which Gen Y employees feel like colleagues and part of the team, not as novices or apprentices, will encourage idea sharing and open dialogue. This ultimately leads to inventive ideas arising from the employee base.

- The organizational and management structure needs to be simple and lean, focused on providing appropriate support and direction without micro-managing (micro-managing will discourage employees from initiating ideas and impede them moving forward).

- Allow for reasonable risks to be taken and be deliberate about how the organization responds to failures. If risks are rewarded and encouraged even when failures occur, Gen Y employees will continue to flex their creativity and solutions orientation.

- Allow for ideas to flow freely through all levels of the organization – both top-down, bottom-up and across. Ask the question: "Are your employees encouraged with the freedom and opportunities to express their ideas freely?" An open forum will encourage collaborative work at all levels of the organization.

- Gen Y values teams over the individual. Encourage cross-functional teams, projects and social activities to break down silos and foster networking, interactions and exchange of ideas and insights. This will fuel creativity and innovation through initiatives, positive approaches to challenges, collaboration and camaraderie.

- Get down to real business; Gen Y values and is drawn to the entrepreneurial spirit. By focusing on real business problems and encouraging them to contribute to solutions, they will tackle the challenge.

You would think that technology companies would have an advantage in attracting and retaining Gen Y talent over more traditional businesses. However, even this industry is not immune to the overpowering need within the Gen Y DNA to innovate. The "old Silicon Valley" has recently seen annual employee attrition rates rise dramatically in the under 30-year-old category. Employee retention for this group ranges between 70-80%. Compare this with companies such as Google that can attract the best young talent and retain them with attrition rates that are remarkably close to zero. In recent years, there are many companies that have been showcased within popular publications for practices such as carving out time in their employees' schedules where they are encouraged to simply think and develop new ideas or making available a day each week for employees to pursue a project and allowing them to develop and innovate without intervention from management.

Creating these opportunities for Gen Y to innovate is imperative for engagement, employee retention and business growth.

3. Location and Schedule Flexibility

It will be instructive to examine this subject through the eyes of our fictional characters and their challenges in the work environment; particularly where Tyler mentioned to Michelle that he felt he would be more productive if he worked a number of days from home:

The request surprised Michelle. She had always operated a more formal work environment with standard business rules where these types of perks came with proven results and tenure.

Michelle has the difficult task of leading and aligning her organization and adapting to a growing generation of "Tylers" who expect, or at the very least strongly desire, flexibility as part of their work structures. Her instincts say to toe the party line and inform him that he will be considered for flexible work options after he has been with the company for a longer period. At the same time, she is concerned that this might result in Tyler losing some enthusiasm for his role.

She approaches her boss James, a 30-year veteran of the company, to get his views on the work-from-home request. Michelle is actively positioning herself to replace James when he retires and is cautious about making any arbitrary decisions that he would not support. His reaction is an abrupt, "No". James centralized his departments a decade earlier so that all of the employees could be in the same office and has always felt more comfortable with his entire employee base being present. He contends that employees who work from home have too many distractions and it is too difficult to put control mechanisms in place to ensure they are being productive. As a Baby Boomer, James' perspective is very indicative of his generation.

Recently, Tyler really impressed Michelle. He came to her and explained how their business unit could save a lot of time spent on data entry if they created online forms. Tyler laid out the entire plan on how he could spearhead this project and develop the forms himself; he would need only her support in appealing to their IT department to set them up on the company website with the appropriate workflows. He also took time over several nights and weekends to create mock-ups of the forms and emailed them to her. He seems very passionate about how much time and effort this will save.

While the example is intentionally simplified in order to illuminate the point, Michelle's dilemma is extremely common for today's business leaders. She is balancing at the fulcrum between the drivers that will engage Gen Y and the traditional business structures that have not yet abundantly adjusted to these drivers.

For those leaders that are skeptical about telecommuting in general, consider a recent experiment conducted by Nicholas Bloom, a professor of Economics at Stanford University.

Bloom worked with Ctrip, a NASDAQ-listed, 16,000-employee travel agency in China. Ctrip executives were contemplating work from home options but had held off due to the typical leadership concerns. A large majority of Ctrip's employees were young and in their first professional roles within a business. They conducted a nine-month trial where over 100 service employees were provided the opportunity to work from home while their productivity and quality of work was assessed carefully. The results surprised everyone at Ctrip:

"First, the performance of the home workers went up dramatically, increasing by 13% over the nine months of the experiment. This improvement came mainly from a 9% increase in the number of minutes they worked during their shifts (i.e. the time they were logged in to take calls). This was due to reductions in breaks, time off, and sick days taken by the home workers. The remaining 4% improvement came from home workers increasing the number of calls per minute worked. In interviews, the workers attributed the increase in time worked to the greater convenience of being at home (e.g. the ease of getting tea/coffee/lunch) and the increased output per minute to the relative quiet at home.

The overall impact of WFH was striking. The firm improved total factor productivity by between 20% to 30% and saved about $2,000 a year per employee WFH. About two thirds of this improvement came from the reduction in office space and the rest from improved employee performance and reduced turnover."

"Does Working From Home Work?
Evidence From a Chinese Experiment"
Quarterly Journal of Economics
oxfordjourals.org at Stanford University
Nicholas Bloom
March 3, 2015

Again, the rapid advancement of high-speed mobile connectivity and available applications has made the practical constraints around telecommuting a non-issue. Instant messaging, web-based meetings, email, online collaboration, etc.: all enable employees within organizations to realistically complete their work from virtually anywhere in the modern world. So, why is it that North American industry has not yet altogether embraced the concept of mobile workers?

In 2014, only 2.6% of the American workforce, or 3.2 million workers, worked a majority of their time from home according to statistics from the American Community Survey. Conversely, home workers made up 13.9% of all those at work in the UK during the first quarter of 2014. It would seem that the United States is lagging behind the rest of the developed world in terms of this inevitable trend.

This statistic is perplexing in many ways. Those in the Baby Boomer and Gen X categories are, for the most part, technically savvy enough to recognize benefits and take advantage of mobile working. But why are US-based businesses so reluctant to make it policy with these same Boomers and Gen Xers holding the prevalent share of leadership roles? There are a number of factors which contribute to this reluctance, including the following:

- Control: There is a general unwillingness to fully enable remote working and flexible schedules due to apprehension that performance will suffer without having the direct daily contact that comes with the office environment.

- Tradition: Some employers persist in clinging to outdated norms and viewpoints that suggest face-to-face contact is "better" for employees, despite the significant number of immediate communication channels available today which did not exist even one short decade ago.

- Value: Whether or not they freely admit the fact, today's leaders – predominantly Boomer and Gen X – evolved through careers in environments which highly valued symbols of corporate status: consider the corner office and its implication of higher importance. It is difficult for them to change this engrained value perspective.

The reason for the low rate of adoption when compared to other advanced economies is also likely related to different experiences in execution of a mobile-working strategy. As David Lewis, President and CEO of Operations, Inc. illuminated for a recent eCornell webinar entitled 'Lead Your Remote Workforce To Success':

"After Yahoo and BestBuy dissolved their remote work programs in 2013, many business leaders and HR professionals started looking at their own flexible work programs with a keener eye and a greater degree of skepticism and scrutiny.

But remote work as a business practice is not inherently problematic; it's that most organizations don't know how to make it work to their advantage. When structured properly, a remote workforce can be as effective as any on-site organization."

What does Gen Y think about the low degree of mobile options? What do they value?

"For Gen Y, work is a significant part of their life, but they don't compartmentalize it like some other generations. Physical spaces are pretty meaningless to Generation Y, making telecommuting a desirable option for them. Yes, their work style is very different. Whether it's right or wrong is a whole different debate, but the fact is they're the up-and-coming generation".

"Worklife Flexibility Is #1 Job
Requirement for Generation Y"
Maria Lawson
www.epmsonline.com
February 13, 2013

For Gen Y, this subject does not just cover working-from-home. They make the distinction of truly *mobile* working and it is an important one. Mobile means flexibility – at home, at the coffee shop and at the office. Getting the work done is what they value, not putting in face time at the office. Many of the remote working policies that companies have put in place come with a myriad of restrictions. These are going to require some rethinking for those companies that want to attract and retain the best Gen Y talent.

Of course, not every business can enable every one of their employees to be mobile at all times. This is where flexibility comes in. Every organization needs to evaluate:

✓ Which roles are ideal for mobile working
✓ Which can be 100% mobile
✓ Which are ideal for occasional or regular remote work options

Most leaders will find that the majority of job functions provide for some form of hybrid arrangement that includes mobile and office time.

And what about flexibility in scheduling? The common reaction to this from today's leaders reveals a similar skepticism, or in some cases, outright anxiety. There is a concern around loss of control leading to widespread performance challenges. Again, it is a matter of taking different pragmatic approaches and defining where flexibility can be applied. There are some industries that require more regimented schedules for their employees. For example, most contact centers operate through workforce management software which optimizes schedules based on inbound call volume patterns. It would be challenging to meet customer service demand without these more scientific scheduling schematics. In this type of situation, many companies have moved toward mobile work solutions and flextime for employees. In other instances, smaller service business units can take a team self-management approach (discussed in detail in Chapter 7) where they determine schedules between themselves and are measured as a team to ensure key metrics and objectives are met.

For those situations where mobile options are not feasible and Gen Ys are actually in the office, again changes need to be considered. They are not inclined to collaborate in formal meetings, but rather through social interaction. How often do business professionals sit in a meeting room with the majority of participants either having their laptops open or are madly typing on their smartphones? What does this tell us? It confirms that today *collaboration happens electronically the majority of the time, even when participants are sitting a few feet away from one another.* The modern office, and the one most conducive to Gen Y productivity, is one that limits closed offices and replaces them with open spaces and areas to foster social connections among co-workers. Such an environment encourages brainstorming and cooperation instead of formal boardroom-style meetings, thereby allowing an open, unthreatening exchange of ideas. In a June 2, 2015, interview conducted by Ladan Nikravan (editor of *Chief Learning Officer* magazine), Carik Keogh (CEO of ESIErgonic Solutions) spoke extensively about what Millennials need within their physical work environments to be productive. She included the need for them to have variety of movement, described as "sit and stand" opportunities and noted that Gen Y employees are predominantly bringing their own technology to work (e.g. tablets, iPhones...) and that organizations need to adjust for these changing undercurrents in the workplace.

As we see in the example provided, Tyler does not think twice about working on a weekend because he was focused on the online forms project, not putting in the hours at the office. Many Gen X and Boomer readers will consider this and respond with, "I've worked plenty of weekends to get where I am. What's so different?" The difference is inherent in the statement itself. Boomers and Gen X see long or extra work hours as a means to an end, while Tyler, typical of his generation, sees it as time working on a project about which he is excited. For this reason he would never consider his request to work from home several days per week as audacious or inappropriate. For him, work happens with the goal of moving the project forward whenever, however, wherever.

3.

"I went through interviews at this super-big company and the recruiter said I will probably get an offer later this week. I also interviewed at this small technology company a few weeks ago...I just don't know what I'll do. The big company will provide a good start to my career and the job itself looks interesting. And I really liked the vibe at the technology company. It would be a little less money, I think. They said they worked long hours and it wasn't easy, but they were so laid back and even had a gaming station in the break room where they told me they have weekly competitions on Friday afternoons. That seems like a cool place to work."

23 year old recent
university graduate
Generation Y

Rebranding for Gen Y Talent

Brands that attract Gen Y are powerful. Gen Y will determine where they want to work and where they invest, based on the lens through which they view a company. Millennials are quickly becoming the next dominant group of investors and are likely to be the wealthiest group entering the investment market in history. This has profound implications for business and reinforces the importance of branding that appeals to Gen Y:

"Millennials...control maybe $2 trillion in liquid assets...by the end of the decade that number is expected to surge to $7 trillion. And that will get vastly bigger as Millennials enter their prime earning years and then a massive wealth transfer from their Boomer parents begins."

"The Recession Generation: How Millennials Are Changing Money Management Forever."

Janet Novack and Samantha Sharf

Forbes

August 18, 2014

Throughout the past century, investment along generational lines can be closely correlated to brands that appeal to the values of the prevailing investors of the time. Companies must put emphasis on ensuring their brands resonate with the values of Gen Y as this generation considers where they want to invest their own capital as well as where they want to invest their time within a career.

Even more imminently, the brand has to have this value-based appeal to attract and retain employees. If you are a leader in a large organization and have convinced yourself that dramatic change is not really required to attract and retain Gen Y, consider a recent

Accenture Survey that was covered by CNN Money on May 12, 2015.

"It appears that many Millennials -- that tsunami of future workers -- don't really want to work for you. At least not the newest college graduates. Only 15% of the class of 2015 said they would "prefer" to work for large corporations"

"Where do Millennials want to work?
Not at corporations."
CNNMoney
May 12, 2015

When we look deeper and ask why such a staggering percentage of Gen Y employees are eschewing corporate America, the answer becomes clear: image. Rightly or wrongly, they view large organizations as lagging in terms of developing the work environments and structures that appeal to them. With that said, a handful of large companies have turned the corner in this respect, which is encouraging as it proves they can appeal to Gen Y. Still, the Accenture survey respondents overwhelmingly favored medium-sized companies as preferred future employers. Medium-sized businesses do not have the post-2008 stigma of contributing to the economic downturn and are seen to be progressive, nimble and flexible. This suggests that all companies, irrespective of size, can and should closely consider branding and, in many cases, rebranding.

We will focus on four key areas:

1. Rebranding
2. Recruitment
3. Social Responsibility
4. Full-Life Balance and Fun

1. Rebranding

Future businesses will need to consider **Rebranding for Gen Y** in order to successfully recruit the most talented future employees. Their leaders and HR professionals will need to ensure they implement the right infrastructure to support the promises their brands promote.

For those who believe that investment in enhancing a company's public brand creates less value than investment in other business pursuits, consider this:

"Research from LinkedIn has found that costs per hire can be reduced by 50% and turnover rates lowered by 28% when a company has a strong talent brand in place. On top of this, three-quarters of talent acquisition leaders have said that talent brand significantly increases their ability to hire good talent."

"Five Key Recruitment Trends For 2015"
Ron Stewart
TalentCulture: World Of Work
www.talentculture.com
December 30, 2014

Branding and development of corporate image is more or less a common exercise for almost all corporations. Over the course of the last decade, a trend has begun to take hold where organizations are focusing much more on enhancing their brand specifically to attract and keep top talent within their employee ranks. This is and will continue to be imperative for businesses intent on enticing and retaining employees in the Gen Y category. The challenge is that the brand has to be real. Making it real often requires breaking many of the entrenched Boomer and Gen X beliefs and assumptions that exist within the corporation. It requires the restructuring of policies, internal systems and engrained methodologies and mindsets.

Of course, it is not advisable nor is it pragmatic to discard every traditional business practice or negate core elements of the corporate culture as these have most often been "tried and tested". A delicate balance must be held that appeals to the top talent amongst each generation in the workforce. While the corporate brand cannot be exclusively Gen Y oriented, it is critical that Gen Y be a chief consideration.

"Undertaking a cultural assessment provides insight on where you are today compared with the ideal culture that will support your plan to weather the dramatic shifts taking place in your industry. I am not advocating that companies should change their values annually, but I am strongly suggesting that a cultural assessment as part of that process...will highlight what needs to change to align the workforce

with the strategy while you determine what still holds true as the core of what your company is about."

"Why Your Corporate Culture Is Costing Your Business."
Rita Trehan, Chief Capacity Officer at Rita Trehan LLC
LinkedIn (Linked HR: #1 Human Resources Group)
May 11, 2015

We have established that injecting a healthy dose of branding which appeals to the emerging Millennial workforce is vital. Fortunately, there are a number of best practices which lend themselves to this effort. Branding concepts need to be carefully selected and sincerely absorbed by organizations to attract Generation Y talent. Leaders must focus on what is conceptually important to Gen Y and compare this with their existing image and policies. The difficult task of then precisely intermingling these existing policies and practices comes next. Those Gen Y influencers that represent a fit/balance with existing culture and structure should be adopted.

The authors have suggested a method to take the first step and facilitate this process. It centers on six key brand attributes that must be in place and…

T-E-S-T-E-D

….in order to fortify the brand toward Gen Y preferences. In order to address this practically, assess your own company's brand.

Is it Gen Y **T-E-S-T-E-D**?

Technology: up-to-date, flexible and savvy; tools that ensure speed, balance and convenience. Note that this does not need to be exclusive or restrictive to only technology companies.

Engagement: focus on employee satisfaction – i.e. revenue and earnings placed second to maintaining a social, energetic and above all innovative environment.

Social Responsibility: show that the organization cares for others in addition to the core business pursuits.

Team Drive: highlights interaction with peers and reaffirms the contentment with same demographic employees.

Education: values diverse skills and knowledge in a broad sense and provides for learning opportunity.

Development Focused: supports and encourages career development and growth opportunities including non-traditional means to progression.

It is true that the larger the organization, the more difficult it is to change and rebrand fast enough to keep up with the new generation's preferences. For those that believe this will stabilize at some point, it is time to rethink this outlook. Every time a popular new app becomes established in Millennial popular culture – which occurs at lightning speed – it becomes clear how difficult it is to keep up with the latest trends and preferences of Gen Y. As mentioned earlier, the generations that follow will only add to the variety and speed of change. Even with the **T-E-S-T-E-D** brand attributes, they should be constantly challenged to ensure that the developing brand stays current and relevant. In addition, when considering the whole brand question, it is important to note that many Gen X and some Boomers are now being heavily influenced by the much larger and more dominant Gen Y culture – a dynamic that clearly establishes Gen Y's power in shaping the future. What the Boomers and Gen X sometimes regard as disruptive within a business is actually setting the trend for an environment that is simply focused on productivity and driving results within a neoteric context.

As Paul Dinan outlines:

"Cultivate your secret sauce: A critical starting point involves figuring out what's special and unique about your organization, and how your company's DNA can be attractive to Gen Y. This is the foundation of your employee value proposition. You can blend both who you are today, and who you want to be in the future

to support your vision and business strategy, but it needs to be real. You can't fake it with Millennials. They've been bombarded with advertising and PR messages since before they could walk, and can smell insincerity a mile off. In our experience defining what makes your organization unique requires merging company and employee perspectives. This means finding common threads from a wide variety of information sources including your strategy, vision, values, rewards philosophy, external stakeholders, engagement surveys, employee turnover and exit interview data, industry benchmarking, and of course input and feedback from people across your organization."

"5 Ways To Beat Google, Apple, Facebook for Gen Y Talent"
Paul Dinan
www.tlnt.com
04/05/2012

Through a meticulous evaluation of Gen Y preferences and alignment of these in the redevelopment of a corporate brand, companies will be better suited to recruit top talent from this generation. The methods and tactics utilized in recruiting itself have to change as well, not only to reinforce the brand, but also to continuously draw in high potential Gen Y candidates.

2. Recruiting Generation Y Talent

Many traditional methods of recruiting are quickly becoming obsolete and companies are experiencing an increased obligation to stay on top of the latest recruiting methods to tap into the Gen Y pool. Some of these include:

- Utilizing current social media hot points, such as:
  - ✓ Instagram
  - ✓ LinkedIn
  - ✓ YouTube
  - ✓ Facebook
  - ✓ Twitter
  - ✓ Pandora
  - ✓ Vine

- Creating a web presence that engages current and prospective employees and reinforces the brand with features that appeal to Gen Y. The bolder companies have even developed public social sites that enable prospective and existing employees to engage in online dialogue.

- Sponsoring and participating in targeted events and activities to attract Gen Y talent and utilizing these to create opportunities for prospects to engage in peer interviews and job shadowing.

When examining the list of apps above, it reveals several recruitment channels that have not yet been exploited by business. For example, Vine is a social app that enables sharing of individual video vignettes that are less than six seconds long. It is tremendously popular with Gen Y. Yet, it has not been utilized expansively by companies as a recruitment instrument with reinforced branding.

Another major area of untapped opportunity in this ambit of recruitment: *going mobile*. According to Ron Stewart and *TalentCulture*, 43% of job hunters utilize mobile devices in their search while 59% of recruiters do not deploy mobile-friendly career sites. This divergence is significant and within the Gen Y community the disparity will be even more pronounced. It represents a huge opportunity for businesses that act on it now.

"Reaching young Millennials where they live will be key to recruiting them. And where they live (at least until something better comes along) is their smart phone. Among 2015 grads, 64% said they will use or have used mobile apps in their job search."
"Where do Millennials want to work? Not at corporations."
CNNMoney
May 12, 2015

In a 2011 white paper entitled: "Mobile HR Solutions: Connecting & Empowering Your Workforce" by VDC Research and ADP Research Institute, only 25% of mid-sized companies and 28% of large businesses were reported to have any plans to implement a mobile recruiting capability on smartphones within 18-24 months. The insight that this provides leads to one simple conclusion – mobile recruiting needs to expand.

One of the areas that corporations are slowly becoming more comfortable with is their degree of openness to sharing company information that increases Gen Y responsiveness to recruitment efforts. For those organizations that are still reticent to expose too many details about their inner-workings in order to develop a brand that will appeal to Gen Y candidates, here is something to consider: in today's socially connected world, Gen Y will *always* find a way to access more information than a prospective employee could prior to the proliferation of the Web. Given this reality, sharing more in-depth details about the company in recruiting efforts can bring positive gains. A brand that is synonymous with trust is an important factor for Gen Y.

When it comes to recruiting processes, most companies have shifted almost entirely toward online formats. In a way, this is a case of herd mentality where a majority of organizations follow the leading best practices within their industries. However, the most innovative companies are continually finding ways to be creative and breaking the molds in their appeal to Gen Y top talent.

In 2004, Google placed billboard ads that simply stated "first 10-digit prime found in consecutive digits of *e*) .com". For those who were capable of solving the puzzle and went online to complete it, a secondary puzzle was presented. Once a user solved the second puzzle, they were presented with a message offering them the opportunity to apply for a position in Google labs; an ingenious recruitment campaign to attract the exact math and engineering expertise they required. In a similarly innovative campaign, MasterCard introduced its *#internswanted* social interview. This represented a remarkable shift in their method that involved asking applicants to engage in an open, online discussion regarding the future of their industry; specifically, tackling the future challenges of a cashless consumer world. Not only did this result in Gen Y applicants immediately feeling involved in a key corporate strategy, and thus connecting them to the MasterCard brand, it enabled the company to screen participants for the types of potential candidates they were looking to entice.

As corporations compete for talent, reinforcing their brand through creative and innovative recruitment techniques that appeal to the Millennial population will become increasingly important.

Campus recruiting has seen a noteworthy resurgence as the population of Gen Y graduates has grown. Given the size and supply that Millennials represent and will continue to represent in the upcoming decades, competing for talent by building a strong brand through universities and colleges is essential for tomorrow's corporations. It is common, when thinking about campus recruiting, to picture career fairs with booths and companies handing out swag to soon-to-be graduates. These, in fact, did govern the campus recruiting landscape for decades. Career fairs and on-campus interviews are still a core component to campus recruiting strategies, although contemporary standards require a considerably more digitally sophisticated presentation in individual corporate booths.

As with most other areas, campus recruiting has evolved far beyond the traditional career fair models. Of course, the ever-pervasive technology factor is playing an increasingly important role in this evolution. The powerhouse online recruiting provider, Monster. com, recognized this when the company launched its Monster College platform. They identified a key gap in campus recruiting – namely, a lack of integrated digital connectivity – and through Monster College, partnered with the majority of major corporations as well as thousands of mid-sized firms to connect colleges, hiring companies and students. This type of online connectivity is crucial when trying to identify top talent from within the Gen Y ranks.

As important as strategies to attract new graduates will be, given the astounding number of Gen Ys that will be completing degrees in the coming decade, online recruiting techniques should not be limited to campus recruiting but must be the foundation of a comprehensive recruiting strategy:

"Technology's role in recruitment serves as both a resource to the employer and a benefit to the potential employee. The Internet – social networking websites specifically – makes recruiting convenient for employers and provides valuable information about talented individuals in the workforce. For prospective employees, these websites allow easy access to information about potential employers. Furthermore, this recruitment strategy resonates with Generation Ys desire for flexibility."

"Generation Y in the Workplace"
Brown/Carter/Collins/Gallerson/Giffin/Greer/Griffith/
Johnson/Richardson
The Bush School of Government & Public Service
Texas A&M University
5/7/2010

3. Social Responsibility – A Critical Piece of the Corporate Brand

In April, 2014 The Hartford published results from an extensive survey they conducted with a focus on leadership and Millennials. They found that the definition Gen Y ascribed to leadership was significantly different than that of the other generations. The three most dominant aspects of leadership according to this survey were defined as:

✓ Mentors
✓ Achievers
✓ *Effecters of Change in their Community*

It is extremely telling that what can be summarized as "institutional social conscience" figures so prominently in the Gen Y value system when it comes to assessing the brands they want to patronize or the businesses for whom they wish to work. To ignore this is to deny that accommodating the collective Millennial belief system is vital to an organization's long term survival. Generation Ys are passionate about social issues and the environment. Compared to the views of the Boomers and Gen Xs, economic development takes a backseat. This is not to say that the Boomers and Gen Xs do not care about social issues; they are not as vocal about it and have definitely not held to the guiding principles to the extent that they would leave a well-paying job based on their company's social responsibility level. Gen Ys, conversely, feel strongly about such issues. An organization that does not incorporate corporate citizenship, sustainability and a global point of view will undoubtedly risk alienating this generation, both as customers and employees.

Citing a 2011 study by TBWA/Worldwide and TakePart, Andrew Swinand adroitly captures the magnitude of this necessity:

"It's not just a matter of selling products and services to millennials — corporate social responsibility is, increasingly, how organizations sell themselves to

potential employees. Three in four young adults who say they consider themselves social activists say they seek out employers that support a social cause, according to the TBWA survey. Seeking to align themselves with corporations that are attempting to give back to the world is very much a part of their career calling."

"Corporate Social Responsibility is Millennials New Religion".
Andrew Swinand
Crain's Chicago Business
March 25, 2014

Most leaders do not need a roadmap to figure out where employees can participate in charitable or other related causes. Many corporations have a variety of causes in which they publicly support and invest. Some leading-edge best practices that a number of corporations have adopted warrant consideration:

- Encourage social responsibility in the self-development components of employee performance objectives.

- Provide "paid days" where employees can take time off in order to volunteer at a charity of their choice.

- As a component of overall compensation, provide an annual stipend that employees use to donate to an NPO or charity.

- Acknowledge and recognize employees publicly for specific contributions to social responsibility.

- A critical piece – the social network! Connect employees with similar or matching social cause interests, enabling them to align and develop their own initiatives.

Whenever possible, it is important to provide these as options and (with the possible exception of inclusion in performance objectives) that the company does not mandate participation in specific contributions. The moment you mandate, you take the fun out of it for Generation Y. Since Millennials seek and appreciate the opportunity to make a positive difference in society and the world, give them some runway and their contributions will be noteworthy. The positive publicity that your organization will gain is priceless.

A major part that contributes to the social responsibility sum is diversity and inclusion. While many leading CHROs and CEOs have incorporated increased diversity and inclusion measures into their organizations, many other corporations lag. In addition, many have made claims of diversity that are not backed up in action. All it takes is a web-search of a company's top leadership positions to verify if they are "walking the talk" that is professed around diversity and inclusion. "Inclusion" is superseding diversity as the neoteric all-encompassing definition for leveraging multiplicities of skills, backgrounds, orientations and experiences.

In fact, a 2014 report on Human Capital trends by Deloitte indicated that an overwhelming majority (80%), while acknowledging the importance of diversity as a strategic business imperative, did not consider their organization ready to address the issues of diversity and inclusion. Perpetuating this lack of action around diversity and inclusion will result in missed opportunities and economic decline for those corporations that do not hastily ameliorate the inherent insufficiency it will create. Gen Y exists in the era of globalization where inclusion is not only accepted, it is a necessity for continued growth of any business. There is no room in the Gen Y psyche for practices or policies of exclusion or marginalization in the business environment. Companies must not only make diversity and inclusion key ingredients of their brands, they must live the behaviors implied in the promises of the brand.

4. Full-Life Balance and Fun

When further considering the need for leaders and HR professionals to tailor their brand toward Gen Y predilections, it is important to consider what has customarily been referred to as work-life balance. This term has become somewhat cliché and overused in the past decade and it has fallen under some cynical criticism as suggesting a diminution of work effort. This directly contravenes the Boomer and Gen X psychology when it comes to issues surrounding their views on work ethic, and creates a point of conflict with the newer Gen Y entrants to the work environment. To Gen Y, the desire to work for companies that support a real blend between work expectations and personal life is clear-cut.

As Stephanie Armour points out:

"Work-life balance isn't just a buzz word. Unlike boomers who tend to put a high priority on career, today's youngest workers are more interested in making their jobs accommodate their family and personal lives. They want jobs with flexibility, telecommuting options and the ability to go part time or leave the workforce temporarily when children are in the picture."

"Generation Y: They've arrived at
work with a new attitude".
Stephanie Armour
USA Today/Money
November 8, 2005

The corporate brand needs to purposefully contemplate this reality. A derivative form of the conventional work-life balance – full-life balance – is an engrained Gen Y value and must be part of the brand and practice of today's and tomorrow's companies.

What is *full-life* balance? It is simply inclusive of all elements of a contemporary individual's existence: work, social, family, experiential. The Gen Y psyche contemplates an ideal equilibrium between these factors as opposed to a binary equation of merely two portions.

Then there is the element of fun. Leaders who incorporate elements of fun and make their work environments places where employees can enjoy themselves, be entertained and be social will flourish with Gen Y. This is a factor that pertains to all employees. In some ways, the brain is similar to a muscle: it is meant to work hard and then relax for a moment. If a muscle is worked without a period of repose it will eventually deteriorate and become less productive. Allowing and encouraging a fun environment relaxes the brain and then it returns to a focused activity with more alertness and adeptness.

Gen Y is the video game generation. And remember, fun does not mean slacking off. In fact, most studies show that it enhances productivity. It can range from play centers in break rooms, team pods, collaboration corners/standing areas where colleagues can discuss work challenges and solutions. A casual work environment (dress code, working styles, communication styles/methods) provides a relaxing environment where creativity can thrive. Google, in many ways the benchmark of Gen Y employee engagement, encourages casual dress, rock climbing walls and video games in its environment.

This promotion of fun in the workplace has become a celebrated and pivotal part of their corporate branding.

To conclude the brand discussion, developing a brand that addresses the values and prerequisites of employment within Generation Y will only grow as a key imperative for any business leader, HR professional or company competing in the global talent pool of the twenty-first century.

4.

"I'm up to a Gold Expert level on our company 'Ask a Peer' network. I've provided over 145 answers to fellow employees around the world over the past 6 months. Not only does my profile on the company portal have the gold seal beside my name, our Senior VP actually noticed when I made Gold and sent me an instant message to thank me. That was cool. He suggested I provide links to our Knowledge Base in some of my longer responses on 'Ask a Peer' and said I could be at Platinum in no time!"

31 year-old
service center team lead
Generation Y

Recognition is the New Currency

A lot of commentary has been made around the degree of narcissism that is often associated with Gen Y by the older generations. The argument is simple: this is the generation where everyone who grew up in organized sports received a ribbon for participating. It is the generation who grew up with helicopter parents. It is the generation that adopted Facebook, the ultimate "all-about-me" online vehicle and then just as quickly added other applications focused on self. It is the selfie generation. The viewpoint is that the Y Generation is more narcissistic than their predecessors as a result of the focus on them as the center of the universe since a young age.

In fact, there may be some evidence of this drift toward a greater collective egocentricity. The University of Michigan Institute for Social Research undertook a study that analyzed data on empathy among nearly 15,000 college students over three decades. The results were most recently presented in 2010 at the annual meeting of the Association for Psychological Science.

"'We found the biggest drop in empathy after the year 2000,' said Sara Konrath, a researcher at the U-M Institute for Social Research. 'College kids today are about 40 percent lower in empathy than their counterparts of 20 or 30 years ago, as measured by standard tests of this personality trait.'

Konrath conducted the meta-analysis, combining the results of 72 different studies of American college students conducted between 1979 and 2009, with U-M graduate student Edward O'Brien and undergraduate student Courtney Hsing."

This suggests that the notion of Millennials as more self-centered has some factual validity.

"'It's not surprising that this growing emphasis on the self is accompanied by a corresponding devaluation of others,' O'Brien said. The authors concede that there is a growing trend towards self-absorption that is 'accompanied by a corresponding devaluation of others'".

"Empathy: College Students Don't Have
As Much As They Used To."
http://ns.umich.edu/new/releases/7724,
May 27, 2010

An entire chapter could be devoted to this growing tendency and how to move to address empathy in the workplace. For the purposes of this guide, it is illuminated in order to directly address it as a fact of life in the emerging workforce. If it is reality, and it appears this is the case, it needs to be recognized and tackled. This may seem in contrast to the Gen Y preference to operate in groups and their heavy emphasis on peer opinion and social connection. Their esteem of social responsibility and a common attenuation in empathy also seems incompatible. The characteristic of selfishness is incompatible with this at first consideration. However, in these cases it is important to differentiate between selfish and self-centered. Gen Ys are in fact, self-centered, meaning they possess a magnified sense of self and self-focus, while at the same time valuing social connectedness. While they do appear to have a lower degree of inherent empathy at the individual level, their empathy extends to a more macro and global level of social awareness and tolerance.

The reaction of the preceding generations to the level of self-centeredness in the collective Millennial psychology is often one of resistance; in other words, not acquiescing to youthful individualism and the selfie culture. It may help to consider that, in many ways, it really is not the accountability of Gen Ys themselves for the development of this generalized characteristic, but their parents. Parents have enabled what is often referred to as "Generation Me" and they continue to do so. Recently, *Bank of America* and *USA Today* completed a survey of 1000 Millennials and produced the "*Better Money Habits Millennial*" *Report*. The report revealed that even in 2014/15, parental enablement of 18-34 year-olds was prevalent.

"With 35 percent of millennials receiving regular financial support from their parents or other family members, is this the new normal for the millennial generation? Eighty percent of those who receive support regularly said they "know a lot of friends their age" who are getting help from parents and 55 percent of those who receive financial help openly and honestly discuss it with their friends."

Bank of America/USA Today
Better Money Habits Millennial Report
April, 2015

The following chart, taken from data in the aforementioned report, plots where parents of Gen Ys continue to provide financial funding:

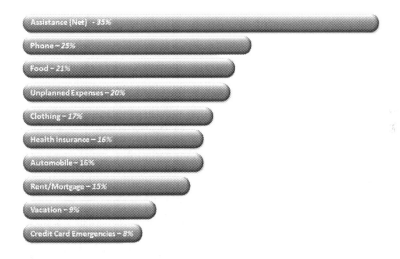

Assistance (Net) – 35%
Phone – 25%
Food – 21%
Unplanned Expenses – 20%
Clothing – 17%
Health Insurance – 16%
Automobile – 16%
Rent/Mortgage – 15%
Vacation – 9%
Credit Card Emergencies – 8%

In a related article in *USA Today*, Hadley Malcolm points out that:

"…many parents appear more than willing to help. More than 30% said they help their kids financially… and 23% said it's because they feel it is their responsibility to step in."

"Mom and Dad: A Financial Buoy"
Hadley Malcolm
USA Today - Money
April 21, 2015

Over 47% of the parents surveyed indicated that they either provide the support without ever having asked their Millennial(s) if it is wanted or after the Millennial(s) have refused the help. This demonstrates the degree to which parents have and continue to enable their Gen Y offspring in North America.

In addition, Yahoo Hotjobs surveyed over 1000 Millennials and discovered that 25% consult with their parents regarding employment decisions.

Let us admit that Gen Y is considerably more self-centered due in large part to parental facilitation. What does all of this have to do with Gen Y in the workplace? Put simply, it means that their needs are drastically different. Parental consultation and involvement has been woven into the fabric of their youth and now adult lives. Their need for guidance and advice supersedes that of previous generations; and, by extension, their need for recognition, consultation and feedback.

To emphasize this point, a recent poll was conducted by the authors utilizing an equal number of recent university graduates and professionals who were over 40 years of age in mid-level to senior management roles. A single question was asked with a frequency matrix to enter their answers:

How often did you correspond (email, text, phone or meet) with your advisor(s) during your time at university?

The results are telling:

- **Forty-one percent** of recent graduates indicated they corresponded with their advisor a minimum of two times per semester throughout their university degrees.
- **Twenty-nine percent** indicated they corresponded at least once every year.

And, those in the comparative (over 40) cohort?

- **Fifty-seven percent** indicated they met with a school advisor less than twice in their entire degree program.
- **Eleven percent** had never met with a school advisor.
- **Ten percent** were not even aware that school advisors were available while they were completing their degrees.

The bottom line: Gen Y grew up with support, coaching and feedback. They continue to require and value these.

For the purpose of this guide, recognition includes a broad context of components, including:

1. Rewards
2. Social Recognition
3. Leadership Connectedness as Recognition

1. Rewards

Rewards refer to formal systems within the work environment for employees. While there are a myriad of reward structures within the business environment today, for Gen Y it is important that these rewards be performance-based. Often reward programs within organizations are overly focused on *effort* as opposed to *results*.

As previously discussed, Gen Y is focused on the end result. Rewarding effort is similar to valuing time in the office; it does not hold inherent meaning for the average Gen Y. Correlating results to performance through formal rewards represents the most viable strategy when Gen Y engagement is the objective. Even today, a large portion of formal reward programs still focus heavily on traditional tenure-based service awards. This is not weighted favorably by Gen Y who is more focused on contributing to results. Where possible, reward structures should be concentrated on this principle and related to "big picture" profitability or business outcomes. For example, in a service environment, developing a rewards and recognition structure focused on upselling of additional services that go directly to the top line and improve customer retention would resonate well with Gen Y. The relevance of the outcomes to company results in this type of a structure can be clearly delineated.

Actual rewards themselves can be varied. It is critical to take the pulse of which rewards will be valued by the employee base. Again, with this generation, while compensation is a motivator, additional rewards are often seen as equally valuable. For example, flex time, gas cards, redeemable points systems, travel dollars, etc. along with many other non-monetary items represent viable rewards as part of a formal structure. For example: just Google "employee recognition" and you will be presented with a wealth of ideas for reward and recognition programs and ideas.

2. Social (Peer-to-Peer) Recognition

Think about the average 19 year-olds today and how prevalent social and peer recognition is in their lives. In many ways, their self-worth is derived from *followers* and *likes* on Instagram, *followers* on Twitter, *subscribers* to YouTube channels, etc. Considerable value is placed on recognition from peers and the public, and it is a perpetual dynamic in the "always on" world of social media for Gen Y. Companies that have recognized the shift in their present and future workforce needs have embraced this and implemented peer-to-peer recognition programs that emulate social media constructs.

As Andrea Doyle points out:

"Gen Y…is adding to the popularity of peer recognition programs. This group is used to getting immediate feedback on what they do".

"The Pressing Case of Peer-to-Peer Recognition"
Incentivemag.com
Andrea Doyle
March 18, 2013.

Peer-to-peer recognition programs have gained more popularity over the past several decades. The majority of these are relatively rudimentary, typically involving a nomination process where peers nominate each other for quarterly or monthly awards. While these satisfy the provision of peer-based recognition, they entail a host of flaws when attempting to apply to Gen Y. The most notable drawbacks are:

- Frequency limitations – Recognition is constricted to once per month or once per quarter and, thereby, the number of employees that can be recognized is constrained.

- Subjectivity – The nominations are often based on the opinions or peer relationships and the selection criteria and process are typically cryptic and unclear.

- Scope limitations – There is limited opportunity for employees to both give and receive individual or team recognition based on the totality of worthy results or outcomes; reducing the recognition opportunities to examples.

- Timeliness – Recognition is often provided days or months after the activity, accomplishment or behavior being rewarded which dilutes its meaningfulness.

A peer-to-peer recognition structure that will resonate with Gen Y is one that is designed as "social recognition". This means that it is entirely inclusive of the organization and acknowledges any employee that earns it. To accomplish this, the social recognition needs to be public and in an online or app-based format that is accessible to all employees and utilized constantly. In other words, it needs to follow the exact opposite approach of the "occasional and subjective" models that have dominated conventional programs.

Taking peer-to-peer recognition to a universal, social and digital stage will appeal to the Gen Y employee base and provide delivery in a format with which they are comfortable. Virtual badging, where users of an application receive "badges" for specific items – is deeply engrained in the Millennial psyche. App providers have tuned into this in recent years. As an example, take the application Waze. In this traffic and routing application, users advance to different levels and higher badge status based on distance travelled and the number of times a user reports traffic-related events. The application is entirely user-driven. There are no monetary rewards – only the virtual badges. However, the motivation of users to improve their status would have you believe they were earning dollars. The badge (whether a "Waze Knight" or a "Waze Grown Up") is the goal.

And guess who is using Waze? Gen Y. The chart below, derived from statistics provided by Metricsmonk.com from May, 2015, shows that the highest user group is the 26-35 (30%) age group with the second highest being 19-25 (24%).

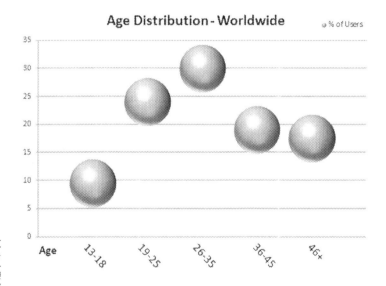

Very few companies seem to have implemented a virtual badging program within their organizations in relation to recognition. Only a portion of those that have created internal online social networks have adopted virtual badging. This is where employees, based on participation, volume of accurate responses, etc., graduate to different "badge" levels within the network. Virtual badging is a highly recommended practice. The social network provides an ideal stage for recognition that connects ideally to the collective Gen Y character.

3. Leadership Connectedness as Recognition

Typically, leadership and feedback do not figure into discussions centered on recognition. In fact, assemble a team of Boomer and Gen X leaders to discuss it and the dialogue will almost invariably lead to groupthink. The non-Millennial business mindset continuously veers toward monetary rewards when considering recognition programs or rewards schema. Yet, there is growing evidence that cash-based incentives are missing the mark. David Peer, president of the Incentive Marketing Association (IMA) proposes that this is because monetary rewards simply do not lead to positive memory formation and, therefore, have little impact on engagement:

"In every single focus group that anyone's ever held to get a bunch of people together and ask them what they want (for an incentive award), 80 percent said cash…but at the end of the day, that has nothing to do with trophy value, it has nothing to do with shared

memory, it has nothing to do with engagement. Why are you asking people what they want when you know what their answer is? Why don't you design something that achieves the objectives you're starting out with for the program?"

'The Continuing Case of Non-Cash Rewards'
www.incentivemag.com
Leo Jakobson
April 4, 2012

Leadership as a form of recognition is intentionally included as a key form of recognition for the purposes of this guide because, in short: it is and will increasingly be one of the most instrumental parts of the equation for the Millennial generation. For Gen Y, it is and will continue to greatly outweigh monetary rewards.

McKinsey & Company conducted research on this very subject in 2009. While the analysis was conducted several years back, the relevance of their findings has only multiplied since 2009 as more and more Gen Ys have found their way into the workplace:

"The respondents view three noncash motivators – praise from immediate managers, leadership attention (for example, one-on-one conversations), and a chance to lead projects or task forces - as no less or even more effective motivators than the three highest-rated financial incentives…the survey's top three nonfinancial motivators play critical roles in making employees feel that their companies value them, take their well-being seriously, and strive to

create opportunities for career growth. These themes recur constantly in most studies on ways to motivate and engage employees.'"

'Motivating People: Getting Beyond Money'
McKinsey&Company - Insights & Publications
Martin Dewhurst, Matthew Guthridge
and Elizabeth Mohr
November, 2009

Gen Y has been receiving coaching and feedback from their parents and other adults their whole lives. This feedback is almost expected once they begin working within an organization. Yet, today most organizations formalize feedback through quarterly or an annual event of job or performance evaluations. This is far too infrequent.

Generation Y wants to feel connected to their leaders. While traditional organizational structures and different levels within companies will continue, the way these levels interact will not.

Providing the opportunity for employees to interact and be connected with leaders and creating a culture that broadly incorporates feedback and connectedness as a form of recognition is paramount to the future sustainability of companies. Leaders being visible, engaged and demonstrably supportive of two-way feedback mechanisms will facilitate the prevalent need for recognition through this type of inclusion within the Gen Y employee base.

So critical is leadership that a 2010 survey published in *The Journal of Human Resource and Adult Learning* found that, along with compensation, it was the most important motivating factor Gen Y considered with regards to their desire to remain employed with a company:

"The categories of "Leadership" and "Salary" were mentioned by each of the respondents. As such these two factors may be considered the two most influential factors and may have the greatest impact on Gen Y employees. The "Leadership" category captured all responses relating to management style...In the "leadership" category, 54% of the respondents asserted that leadership was a motivating component of their work environment. Statements reflecting these positive comments included: "fantastic mentors and supervisors"..."

"Generation Y in the Workforce: Managerial Challenges", The Journal of Human Resource and Adult Learning, Vol. 6, Num.1.

Meier, Crocker, Stephen F.

June 2010

In order to clarify this concept of Leadership as recognition, the authors have chosen to define its foundations as **SMC** or **"Senior Management Connectedness"**. SMC is made of an inventory of four key attributes that leaders need to espouse and implement in their approach to the employee base and most importantly, their Gen Y workers. These are as follows:

SMC Attribute 1: Visibility

First and foremost, leaders need to be visible *online*. This transcends having a monthly business update or an online profile on the company portal. Leaders need to be *actively* online. This means producing blogs regularly, participating in social forums consistently and being frequently available to employees via email and chat applications. Many leaders today go the extra step and make a concerted effort to ensure their employees are connected with them on LinkedIn. Providing an endorsement or recognition in an online social channel such as this will have a profound impact on employee motivation.

Leaders need to be consistently communicating **the big picture**. Gen Ys want to understand their organization from an all-encompassing perspective. They want to understand what is in their CEO's or president's mind in terms of vision and strategy. Spending a given amount of time on live messaging to reinforce leadership availability internally – even if for just an hour or two per week – will pay dividends with employees and particularly with Gen Y employees.

SMC Attribute 2: Accessibility

This attribute is all about encouraging input and providing a critical employee recognition touch point by acknowledging and interacting with employees in response to that input. Gen Y expect a more informal and interactive relationship with all levels of management.

Again, this easily ties back to leveraging technology. Leaders today have a myriad of potential channels to seek out employee input. This can be accomplished, even in global Fortune 1000 companies, through events such as virtual all-employee meetings where leaders take questions in a panel format similar to those often associated with town hall type meetings. Public forums where employees ask leaders written (or even video-based) questions and leaders respond to the entire employee base are ideal for appealing to Gen Y employees. Any vehicle to invite questions openly, share responses and demonstrate true transparency and a common connection to employees increases their sense of being valued and, consequently, recognized.

Accessibility also means increasing the frequency of one-on-one interactions. Imagine the workplace environment in the 1970s where the idea of a front-line employee's planned dialogue with a C-level executive entailed the formality of a rare visit to the head office, one's best suit, and undue stress and apprehension. It would be a BIG event. Fast forward to current day: not only is Gen Y comfortable with the concept of emailing their leaders with a comment or question, they see this as normal. Leaders cannot think in hierarchical terms when it comes to Millennials.

The example above contemplates an employee emailing a senior leader. Digital communication is the primary source of interchange within most corporations today. For someone in the workforce during the 1980s, voicemail and voice interaction was the dominant communication method. Today's employees send and receive many times more emails than they leave and receive voicemail.

As part of its *New Boom series on Millennials in America*, National Public Radio noted:

"We've all heard that automated voice mail lady, telling us what to do after the beep. But fewer people than ever are leaving messages. And the millennials, they won't even listen to them — they'd much rather receive a text or Facebook message."

"Please Do Not Leave A Message:
Why Millennials Hate Voice Mail"
Rachel Rood
www.npr.org
Oct 23, 2014

This extends to the corporation and the work environment. Leaders need to maintain an **Electronic Open Door Policy**. Open door policies have been a prevailing business custom since first introduced by IBM in the 1920s. It is based on the idea that employees can access senior leaders to discuss any individual or general items. There has been considerable debate around the effectiveness of this and whether employees fully trust the concept. An

Electronic Open Door Policy has considerably more efficacy when it comes to the current workplace. With email and instant messaging representing a more comfortable and prevalent communication channel in the workplace, there exists less of an intimidation factor (sending an email to the CEO with a question about business direction has a more unceremonious quality to it compared to a meeting in the CEO's office).

The foundation of an *Electronic Open Door Policy* includes the following best-practices for leaders:

- Demonstrate a willingness to receive emails from employees by encouraging them to contact leaders with ideas, concerns, etc.

- Do not limit or specify the type of input desired. If kept unrestricted 99.9% of employees will not use this opportunity to connect with their leaders on trivial items or those that should go elsewhere.

- Respond to employee emails within a reasonable timeframe using whatever metric you would ascribe to in responding to a customer.

- Provide an online forum where employees can ask questions or provide inputs more publicly and ensure that responses are timely and informative.

- Leverage social media to continually reinforce corporate messages and direction through multiple forms of media as opposed to heavy reliance on email.

SMC Attribute 3: Flexibility

The term "flexibility" can alarm leaders. Ostensibly, flexibility is seen as "loosening of controls". This does not have to be the case. Flexibility involves maintaining an open-minded approach and assessing requests that may, at first, seem unreasonable with a view on how they will impact engagement and overall results. It does not mean acquiescing to every appeal. Because there is an innate tendency for leaders to view the management of younger employees, especially the very unique Gen Y employee, with trepidation, there is a parallel tendency to be wary of increased flexibility.

For leaders to successfully engage Gen Y, they will be required to question the importance of traditional rules, policies and *de facto* standards and assess whether they represent a risk to productivity. These risks then have to be weighed against the risks of a disengaged workforce and the impacts to employee retention and the bottom line. A number of these have been touched upon in the preceding chapters. These include items such as work schedules, mobile work options, office setting and environment. While it seems easy to accomplish, implementing and sustaining real flexibility requires changes in engrained mindsets and norms. A recommendation was made in Chapter 2 that companies will be successful by increasing their innovation focus. This means opening more time and opportunities for younger employees to participate in sharing ideas and even working on distinct projects. While this seems straightforward, there are multiple long-established attitudes within the cultural mien of any large organization that inhibit leaders from executing increased flexibility in these situations. For example, leaders consider how more experienced employees will respond to younger, less experienced peers contributing in special roles they perceive as earned perks? This is a natural concern. But then, imagine a leader who decides not to create opportunities for Gen Y employees to contribute innovatively based on perceived entitlements of older workers – the long-term risk is considerably greater.

In the end, the question leaders need to ask themselves "is it really *that* important?" or "is it really *that* detrimental to the business?" In most instances, they will probably find the answer is "no". It is really not that important that some older employees will be rubbed the wrong way when inexperienced Gen Ys join their project. No, it is not that detrimental to the business if employees have the flexibility to work remotely several days a week. These answers point to where opportunities to boost the extent of flexibility within an organization will manifest themselves.

Current thought leadership in this area suggests that situations such as the above do not require the advent of new business rules. Rather, flexibility comes from the blurring of conventional rules and using a more fluid approach to drive business results.

"Intuitively leaders understand a zeitgeist is changing in the rules of business. 81% of people in our surveys said that 'power today is about influence rather than control.'"

"Tomorrow's Leaders will be Flexible,
Selfless and Ready to Collaborate."
Author: John Gerzema
FastCompany
May, 2013

SMC Attribute 4: Integrity

Leadership integrity encompasses an approach to management that is principled, direct and trustworthy.

As Col. Eric Kail defines it:

"Of all the facets of character, integrity might be the most critical – it builds valuable trust between people – and yet also the most esoteric."

"Leadership character: The role of integrity."
Author: Col. Eric Kail.
The Washington Post
August 8, 2011

Of course, it should be noted that integrity is an important attribute for leaders, period – not just in terms of Gen Y engagement, but also in terms of respect in the work environment overall.

"The many ethical lapses that have sunk organizations illuminate the importance of integrity in top-echelon executives. And that's not just an impression influenced by front-page headlines. Research by the Center for Creative Leadership...shows that integrity is the key criteria in determining success by top executives."

"Why Leaders need to have Integrity."
Author: Harvey Schachter
The Globe and Mail
September 8, 2013

The importance of the integrity factor is amplified within the Gen Y ranks. Millennials grew up watching the fallout of Enron, the 2008 financial crisis which was largely attributed to deregulation of the financial markets and Wall Street greed. Gen Y watched many of their Boomer parents stress over crashing retirement savings while observing the major news networks vilify the organizations that contributed to the recession. They watched executives being hauled off to prison and developed distinct impressions about corporate avarice.

The connected-world Gen Y has grown up in has imbued them with a strong sense of social awareness. In fact, a study by the Intelligence Group published by *Forbes* magazine in January, 2014 found that 64% of Millennials cited "making the world a better place" as a top priority. In short, they will not follow leaders that do not have credibility.

Ashridge Business School conducted a similar survey of over 1000 Gen Y employees:

"The research also showed that Gen Y sought a different set of values such as working for an organization with ethics and integrity; working for an organization committed to social responsibility, and, doing work that is of value to society."

"What do Generation Y really want?"
HRZone
Author: Carina Paine Schofield
July 9, 2014

To further emphasize how important this and the other **SMCs** are to Gen Y engagement, consider the following 2015 survey result:

"A new survey from the Society for Human Resource Management found 72% of employees rank "respectful treatment of all employees at all levels" to be the most important factor in job satisfaction.

The other factors in the top 5 are trust between employees and senior management (64%); benefits (63%), compensation/pay (61%); and job security (59%).

As for the actual work itself? It ranked No. 11."

"What do employees want most? R-E-S-P-E-C-T"
Jeanne Sahadi
CNN Money
April 28, 2015

The factors impacting recognition that we have depicted are numerous and profoundly interrelated. In order to bring them to life using our fictional characters, an example is provided below that incorporates the key concepts as well as several of the **Senior Management Connectedness** factors in order to draw the various concepts together:

James has a problem. His company has just closed the books on their Fiscal Q1 and the business unit that he leads is considerably behind on their major strategic initiative. During the previous fiscal year, the business unit's customer retention dropped from 93% to 92.7%. The department generates several billion in revenue per year so the 300 basis point reduction in retention represents a considerable hit to net income. As a result, the major strategic imperative for the new fiscal was to regain the historical retention rate of 93%.

The plan to recover retention was to start immediately with a root cause analysis that included: a) an examination of reasons for customer churn from the previous year, as well as; b) brainstorming sessions with front-line employees to determine where they felt quality and service could be improved in order to improve retention. James and his senior director, Michelle, had intended to have the analysis wrapped up in the first 30 days of the new fiscal.

Unfortunately, the business unit is now three full months into the fiscal year. The root cause analysis has not been completed and the retention rate for Q1 is continuing to drop. It now sits at 92.5%.

James and Michelle meet to discuss their lagging performance. The issue: a number of key individuals resigned during the first quarter. One was a financial analyst who had done most of the billing and customer reporting. In addition, there were a number of account representatives who left the company during Q1, causing Michelle and her managers to deprioritize the customer-loss analysis while they scrambled to hire new recruits. They are worried that their younger employees are not adapting to the culture. All of the attrition came from employees with less than two years at the company and all under 30 years of age.

During the meeting, they determine that they need to do something drastic to get the retention strategy moving.

Michelle has mentioned many times in the past several months that she is impressed with Tyler. Initially, she told James that she felt he was too entitled and bold in his requests. She felt that he needed to earn his stripes before requesting to get involved in some initiatives and his request to work remotely seemed premature. More recently, however, she has seen him from a different perspective. She did approve him to work limited hours from home on a pilot basis and she was pleasantly surprised. Tyler's performance remained high and he worked on a number of extra improvement projects on his own time. Plus his work was high-quality. She has made sure to let him know that she is impressed and sees increasing opportunity for him to continue his career at the company.

Not knowing how her boss will react, Michelle tentatively suggests to James that she give Tyler a special assignment to gather the employee feedback and collaborate with the new financial analyst to see if they can recover lost time. She half expects James to outright reject the idea as putting something so critical in the hands of a young employee with no tenure seems risky. She is confident, though, that she can give Tyler guidance. Michelle also knows that he is well connected with the employees' wants and needs and, with the majority of their front-line workforce in his demographic, he can probably connect with them effectively.

James' response to the recommendation surprises her. He says, "Whatever it will take to get this back on track – do it!"

Tyler is thrilled at the opportunity when Michelle explains what is needed. He immediately suggests *that they can speed up the employee input process with a simple idea that they begin putting into action right away. Michelle is going to use the business unit's portal to write a blog – something she has been thinking about doing but as of yet has not implemented. She is going to describe the importance of the retention initiative to the business unit and the company. Tyler is going to help her build a feedback icon within the content of the blog where employees will be asked to provide recommendations and ideas on service quality which will go directly to her. Later, they decide that anyone who sends a suggestion will receive an email, copying the entire business unit. They decide that after five days they will assess the ideas and share the most viable with the business unit through Michelle's new blog. There will be a discussion thread added to the business unit's portal where employees can comment on the suggestions presented to further solicit feedback and evaluate the best options. They will then organize a small team of employees from those that have made the most viable suggestions and put them on a special project for implementation. Michelle commits to meet with the special team daily for the duration of the initiative to provide input and direction.*

Michelle ends her day feeling confident that they have a solid action plan that will enable them to recover and focus on the retention initiative.

Michelle's approach to the situation incorporates a number of the key concepts around recognition specific to the Gen Y employee base:

- By entrusting Tyler with this critical project, she not only is providing recognition through **Leadership and Feedback**, she is indirectly building trust with his peers by taking this direction.

- Michelle is adopting the Senior Management Connectivity best practice of **Accessibility** by utilizing technology to solicit feedback directly from employees with her blog. This is also a great example of the **SMC Visibility** factor. With the blog as the conduit, Michelle and Tyler are appealing through the communications channel that the majority of their employees are comfortable with while making Michelle more available and communicative. This is also in line with creating an *Electronic Open Door Policy.*

- The manner in which Michelle and Tyler are responding to input – by openly acknowledging these inputs through emails to the entire base of employees – fits well with the concept of **Social Recognition**. Inevitably, the full team communication technique will lead to **Peer-to-Peer Recognition** as will the ability for employees to openly assess suggestions.

- Michelle and Tyler have also created an ideal reward system by recognizing those employees with the winning ideas by placing them on a special team to implement the solutions. This also represents the SMC attribute of **Flexibility** as Michelle abdicates a great deal of control to the special team.

5.

"We're investing so much time and money in a ton of self-directed training online and our new employees still spend about four to five months in their initial training. We know what it costs to do this, but no one can show me a return on the investment we are making. What makes it worse is that I'm not sure this approach is one where our younger and especially new employees can really learn the way they prefer."

Senior VP for a 400-employee
start-up company
Generation X

Cancel the Classroom:
The New Rules of Learning

Corporate training and education is undergoing a transformation. And it is high time according to many business leaders.

It is estimated that conventional employee training accounts for approximately $100 billion of expense globally. Most CEOs will admit they have very few meaningful metrics in pure dollars and cents when it comes to valuing these mammoth investments. No one, it seems, can articulate a return on investment in real economic terms. Compounding the problem for most large companies includes:

X Widespread redundancies between business units.
X Considerable over-production of unnecessary and unwanted training material.
X Disorganized and unfocused strategy around workforce training priorities.
X Over-investment in outmoded and inefficient new employee onboard training configurations with excessive use of classroom style training.
X Production of online self-learning modules which are often one-dimensional in presentation and narrative which employees reject as patronizing.
X Underuse or non-adoption of advanced interactive technologies and social learning.
X Unsystematic distribution and management of content.

As a 2014 Deloitte survey on *Human Capital Trends* indicated, corporations are considerably behind in revitalizing and modernizing their approach to learning. The following diagram illustrates in grey where they are lagging. The downward arrows represent initiatives or strategies that have either not been started or are considerably behind schedule within global firms:

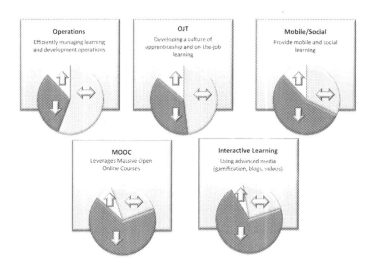

Consider a classic time machine hypothetically for a moment and imagine you are dropped into a typical business 150 years in the past. What would be immediately recognizable? Everything is different: how information moves through the organization, how customers and suppliers interact with the business, logistics and even accounting practices – all have advanced considerably.

Except the classroom!

In many ways, this is true not only within commerce, but within most western pre-university education systems. Progress within learning and education as a whole has been slow. We still put our children in school classrooms where pupils are in desks that face the front and are "served" information by the teacher. Interestingly, we teach the same way in our corporate training rooms, where employees/learners face the trainer – presumably a professional with superior knowledge in the ascribed subject area – and are supplied knowledge.

In recent decades, the only adaptation to this format of learning is virtual training, either through a webinar method or online self-paced learning. These methods have at least leveraged available technologies. The issue is that they are based on the same principles as the largely unaltered classroom: (1) sit in the classroom and listen to the trainer who imparts their knowledge, or (2) observe a screen and listen to the trainer impart their knowledge. Learning remains an absolutely unilateral experience and event for the learner. Most attempts to make online training more interactive fall categorically short of their objective. And the one-to-many lecture-style classroom formats do not enable the real life interactivity required to truly learn effectively.

The strategy debate within most companies has focused on the mix of classroom versus online or virtual training. The outcome of these debates result in efforts toward developing these channels. The argument is limited to two entirely impracticable avenues:

- Online learning is a necessity, but not in the formats delivered today (which are predominantly surrogates for the classroom).

- Traditional classroom training should be practically obsolete now.

Progressive leaders are now more frequently acknowledging the *70:20:10* theory with regards to learning and education:

- ✓ 70% of knowledge and skills are learned on the job through active, short delivery cycle (microlearning) and social learning.
- ✓ 20% are learned from leadership or mentor coaching.
- ✓ Only 10% are learned from traditional classroom or training sessions.

"It is important to realise the 70:20:10 strategic model emerged from a view of modern adult learning that is wider than 'blending'. 70:20:10 draws on the fundamental changes that have occurred, and are continuing to occur, in the workplace. Work is becoming more complex. We work more in teams and rely on others to get our work done more than ever before. Experiential and social learning are

becoming more critical day-by-day as agents of development."

"70:20:10 – Beyond the Blend"
Charles Jennings
charles-jennings-blogspot.com
May 6, 2015

This is where the concept of **Leaky Knowledge** has its roots. **Leaky Knowledge** is as simple as it sounds; it represents the amount of lasting and sustainable knowledge that is not retained, or lost as a result of legacy training and learning practices. Corporations today are spending millions on delivery methods that result in the exact opposite of their intended objective to create knowledge or develop skill. Ninety percent or more of training within today's businesses is delivered through unilateral self-directed online learning or traditional classroom-based. Based on the *70:20:10* model, this is only netting 10% retained cognition. In other words, the job-related information that businesses are attempting to instill in their employees through today's training techniques is escaping into thin air before it can be retained. Archaic learning methods still in use today, in fact, counteract knowledge retention and consequently miss the mark entirely. This gap will grow exponentially if these antiquated approaches continue to be applied with Gen Y. What is the ultimate subsequent result of this high degree of **Leaky Knowledge? Leaky Profits!**

Consider what adult learners have been shown to retain only three days after a training event. That number is a staggering 10%. This equates to only six minutes of every hour of training delivery that is actually retained. Think about the content in your organization's learning catalogue. Which part of the critical knowledge transfer can you afford to waste? Today, it is very likely that your organization is squandering 54 minutes of every hour of training invested!

Another important consideration is that the 90% of non-retained material is only the tip of the iceberg in terms of where **Leaky Knowledge** is occurring. Beyond the wasted expenses in low knowledge retention from traditional classroom or unilateral self-directed training, both the hard and soft costs to develop learning material itself further add to the drain on ROI. It is estimated that instructor-led learning can take an average 40-50 hours of development for one hour of learning. Some course development can be done in less time while others can double if not triple the time to develop.

When we start to add up the cost of developing a 40-hour learning event, the cost of learners to attend, then add the overhead costs to run the event and finally add the related opportunity costs – the reaction should be one of absolute sticker shock!

Multiply the costs above by the multitude of daily classes being run in the average large organization and the lopsided equation reveals that globally, billions are being spent today to develop and deliver learning material which is resulting in about 10% cumulative knowledge retention.

Fixing this represents not only a necessity for companies in preparation for the Gen Y influx; it also presents a massive financial opportunity.

The future of learning, and the only one that will function with Gen Y, includes a much wider plethora of variegated activities and delivery methods. It is incumbent upon business leaders and HR professionals to lead the learning transformation toward a *Maximized Assimilation of Knowledge* approach. While this sounds complex, it is actually a basic arrangement of blended learning systems. A *Maximized Assimilation of Knowledge* approach is derived from the three cornerstones of transferable learning and is deeply applicable to the Gen Y learner. It must:

1. Be Adaptive to Learning Styles
2. Apply On the Job Learning
3. Employ Microlearning and Social Network Knowledge-Sharing

1. Learning Style Adaptation is Critical

Of key importance when transforming learning and training approaches to appeal to Gen Y is the concept of individual learning styles.

For the past five decades, a substantial amount of debate and dialogue has focused on the fact that a learner will process and retain knowledge in different ways. It is widely accepted that there is no single common presentation or delivery type that is suited to a mean statistical average of the population. Over the years, a variety of learning style archetypes have been proposed. These include:

✓ The cognitive attitude approach which scales a learner's mannerisms and preferences.
✓ The NASSP model which breaks learning styles into cognitive, affective and physiological foundations.
✓ The Honey and Mumford cyclical model which focuses on the behaviors of Activist, Reflector, Theorist and Pragmatist.
✓ The Learning Modalities theory which concentrates on perceptual inclinations of learners.

What all of these have in common is that they concede and incorporate the fact that there clearly is a diverse range of learning styles.

The most broadly accepted learning style standard is that of Neil Fleming's VARK model first introduced in 1987. The VARK model defines learning styles through representational systems based on neuro-linguistic programming. It categorizes learning preferences into Visual, Auditory, Reading/Writing and Kinesthetic. More recently the concept of multimodality has been added to the VARK model. Multimodality accounts for learners with the flexibility to adapt their learning styles within two or more of the primary VARK standards.

In general, here is how the VARK standards are broken down:

- ✓ Visual learners process through seeing and training techniques include highlighting in text, symbols, charts and diagrams, visual reminders and color-coding.
- ✓ Auditory learners learn through listening and benefit from recorded sessions, discussion and reading notes or text aloud.
- ✓ Read/Write learners are those that retain knowledge by writing detailed notes, reading text, participating in written exercises, multiple choice quizzes and arranging words into hierarchies.
- ✓ Kinesthetic learners digest knowledge through touching, moving and doing. They operate best in learning delivery environments that encourage moving around, activity and hands-on learning such as models and experiencing activities.

It is recognition of these individual learning styles that drives the need for blended and adaptive delivery methods. Placing employees into the mode of learning dominance that lines up with their natural learning style sets them up to absorb and retain knowledge.

The learner quickly intakes information without the struggle of having to filter through the style of learning that is being presented, and subsequently being forced to filter through the information according to their preferred method. Media utilization needs to be accessible in multiple formats. It is not acceptable to have a situation where one training item is delivered in a singular delivery mode and another in a different format. All training needs to be developed to suit all learning styles.

As an example, consider a simple task of putting together a desk from Ikea. Two decades ago, there was really one option – read the paper instructions provided in the package. This is where most corporations are mired today – single, limited options to deliver the required knowledge and information to complete the objectives. For the most part, this method would appeal to a Visual learner since the assembly instructions are usually limited in text and involve pictorial representations for each stage. The Auditory, Read/Write and Kinesthetic are going to face challenges in building the desk. This is also paralleled in businesses today. The single mode approach leaves a large percentage of the employee base that is being trained with challenges to adapt to the single learning style presented.

Using this same example today, things are different:

✓ The Auditory or Visual learner can go on YouTube or Ikea's own website and listen to/

watch a video with clear instructions on how to assemble the desk.
- ✓ The Read/Write learners can access websites such as apartmenttherapy.com or a social media site and get full-text written step-by-step guides.
- ✓ The Kinesthetic will likely pull up a similar video and (taking frequent breaks to play with the Allen key and parts) will experiment with the tools to try and figure out how to put it together through trial and error.

In the end, no matter the preferred style, the user ultimately selects which style of media they turn to in order to reach their end goal.

This is where a divergence occurs when contrasting the Ikea desk scenario to the corporate world. Companies need to create the same sort of mix for their employees to learn. If this is considered in terms of **Maximized Assimilation of Knowledge** – the desk assembly example reinforces the need to be *perpetually available* which suggests a heavy use of online sources. This type of widely available learning that is adaptive to individual learning styles is either entirely absent or so infrequently practiced that it is nearly indistinguishable in today's learning programs within the business environment.

An additional point of interest to contemplate regarding Gen Y and learning styles: a 2014 study of university medical students in the Millennial category revealed an interesting statistic - 86.8% of the students were determined to be multimodal learners with only 13.8% being identified as unimodal within a specific VARK learning style. What is the most compelling aspect of the study is that it also revealed a prevalent learning style:

"The commonest learning preference was the bimodal category...auditory and kinesthetic being the highest preference. Visual mode had the lowest overall score."

"Understanding your student: Using the VARK model"
Ivan James Prithishkumar
Journal of Postgraduate Medicine
April, 2014

Millennials have been *doing* more than *viewing* their entire lives. Many Boomers and all of Gen X grew up on television and later personal computers; Gen Y grew up on interactive video games and simultaneous multi-channel communications. It is not surprising that their learning styles have advanced to be largely multimodal and slanted toward kinesthetic. And this is why it is also advised that learning experiences enable Gen Y learners to "jump around" between modalities. However, learning in most businesses today is still being developed and delivered with very linear and single-modality techniques.

2. Learning Through On the Job Application

Within effective learning design, the learning material that is provided needs to reflect information that is going to be utilized the most during normal job functions. This is where most training and learning organizations fall short. There is a tendency to present a plethora of knowledge which often includes knowledge the student will rarely need during day-to-day job functions. In reality, for those job elements that are exceptions or arise only sporadically, students fair better simply by being shown where to research critical knowledge in order to handle these situations.

This approach of developing training that gives learners everything they might need to know relies on the participants to sift through large quantities of information and come to a self-derived form of comprehension. This is the big miss in most learning development and application as it does not take into consideration the real world experience of the employee. By taking the all-encompassing "data dump" approach to learning, most businesses do not realize they are indirectly creating *Leaky Knowledge.* This has to be fixed for Gen Y as the Millennial way of processing information does not allow for the provision of superfluous material.

How can this be corrected? There are two key strategies that ameliorate the failures of today's established approaches and help progress the organization toward a **Maximized Assimilation of Knowledge** for the Gen Y learner. These entail:

- Designing learning on the basis of what is needed on the job.

- Creating learning experiences within the context of the job functions themselves.

The trick to determining what is practically needed to be learned in order for an employee to be effective on the job is to *design backwards*. Top learning organizations now design from the perspective of Gen Y and how they will immediately leverage knowledge. Designing backwards involves starting from a position of learner-centric focus. This means avoiding the familiar process of developing from the perspective of the designer or design team who is/ are usually influenced by their own predispositions, internal politics and tendencies to build on existing materials. Instead, beginning the design process at the point in which the learner would actually begin applying the knowledge within a job function and *building backwards* from that point ensures applicability. The learning is quickly integrated and directly applied on the job. To do this effectively, it requires the instructional designer to become intimate with the real job functions, the day-to-day challenges or inefficiencies related to effectively complete those job functions and the organizational interdependencies required to perform them. Only when this level of understanding is achieved can the process of designing backwards begin. Ideally, at this stage the instructional design process entails the development of learning experiences through manifold delivery channels to instill the actual knowledge needed to perform effectively. Through this process of reverse engineering, the learning experience quickly takes the form of relevant functional emulation as opposed to a situation where learners are fed static and often extraneous material through one-way instruction in a synthetic delivery environment.

A great deal of time and effort is exhausted in training development that repeats or incorporates material widely available on the Internet. It is fair to presume that the vast majority of all human knowledge throughout history is now accessible on the Internet. Why do we still create training that includes rewriting information that is readily accessible in the public domain? This creates redundancy and represents an incongruous outlay of labor in the instructional design process which is inherently cost-intensive. Moreover, Gen Y will access information and knowledge through the path of least resistance. It is unnecessary to add information into training material that can be easily obtained through the Internet.

The second critical cornerstone leading to *Maximized Assimilation of Knowledge* through on the job application involves a heavy focus on active learning. Why is this important? When contemplating the 70:20:10 model it becomes self-evident. 70% of learning happens on the job and another 20% through direct coaching and mentor-based instruction. What is most important for the future workforce is that this is how Gen Y *wants* to learn as opposed to classroom training or tedious self-paced modules. Learning experiences need to be embedded within the work experience itself.

Key elements to on the job learning include pull vs push training, microlearning and availability of social networks to reinforce and create comprehension and skill. These will be covered in greater detail later in this chapter. In terms of on the job learning, coaching is another factor that comes heavily into play. The ultimate learning experience comes from working on real situations and real business problems. When front-line managers invest their time in coaching employees directly, the rate of knowledge retention improves. The time lapse to get to knowledge retention is also shortened. Coaching involves shifting front-line management priorities toward taking more accountability for the knowledge development of their employees. Learning moves from a process where front-line managers expect their reports to attend a training session and come out with the skills required to complete core functions, to one where they actively own the development of their employees. And this is magnified in importance given the previously noted preference Gen Y has for feedback, direct involvement and interaction with leaders within the workplace. For Gen Y, nothing is more advantageous in the learning process than one-on-one instruction in a real world environment.

Active learning requires active management. As companies adapt **Maximized Assimilation of Knowledge** frameworks in their learning strategies, a shift is required within front-line management. As the business world moves to more on the job training, it is incumbent upon front-line management to move from a predominantly metrics-based set of activities to functions that are far more weighted toward employee learning. This is easy to intellectualize but not easy to implement. It means a deliberate mind shift in how business leaders deploy and assess their front-line managers.

Managing the active learning process means knowing where each individual employee is in their development. It also means devising strategies to leverage available learning material and providing post-training support and direct coaching. While many managers believe they coach today, it is often limited coaching around problem areas. It is not a holistic approach that revolves around furnishing the individual employee with diverse learning experiences and real-world preparation.

A key part of active management includes diligent follow-up by managers immediately upon completion of any learning event. This requires the manager to acknowledge the completion of training with the employee and to review their comprehension of the material while also identifying any outstanding knowledge gaps. In addition, practical application of the learning needs to be arranged by the front-line manager with intensive coaching. If managers do not actively complete this post-learning event process, especially with Gen Y, it will result in increased *Leaky Knowledge*. If sufficient practical experience is not gained soon after training, one can expect that the majority of learning will quickly be forgotten in a relatively short span of time.

It would be remiss to discuss on the job applied learning development and the Millennial generation without addressing the recent trend of gamification. Gamification represents an attempt to leverage technology in order to accomplish job-applicable learning experiences. It has been flaunted as the pre-eminent future training method to engage Gen Y in the learning process.

At its core, gamification involves the use of game mechanics, most often in a digital environment, that create a learning experience for the user or player in a non-game related subject. It also extends to real or live work scenarios where game systems are utilized to motivate employees and reach end results. This typically involves an experience design that engages the learner through a storyline, play space and game space which ideally leads them to progressively develop skills. It often includes a competitive element such as leaderboards and point systems as well. It usually involves a context of continual challenge levels so that the learner or user is encouraged to move forward in the game space and increase their knowledge through the process.

Recently, gamification has become somewhat of a buzzword within learning organizations with many examples of training organizations flocking to adopt it into their portfolios. Many of these attempts have fallen flat and have not proven to be the avowed panacea to the many current deficiencies plaguing corporate learning today.

The challenge is most often related to relevance, size and design. The enthusiasm that surrounds the underlying idea has resulted in hastily-developed gamification programs where the game is not relevant to work applications being trained. Early attempts at gamification have also resulted in protracted and convoluted training events – opposite the minimalism of 90-second microlearning standards discussed next. These attempts have erred in that they endeavor to overlay existing training or concepts into a game format. This results in the employee/learner not being invested in the lengthy learning experience or game schematic. The rush to adopt gamification has also meant that initial stabs at it have not entailed the necessary investment in time and planning to create an enriched experience design that engages the learner. Too often the herding to gamification has had adverse effects in that learners have found it to be overly-simplified and not producing the intended or desired results.

"Gamification is currently being driven by novelty and hype. Gartner predicts that by 2014, 80 percent of current gamified applications will fail to meet business objectives primarily because of poor design."

"Gamification Trends and Strategies to
Help Prepare for the Future"
Gartner
November, 2012

When it comes to Gen Y, a number of cases have been made that gamification is the ideal method to deliver training, based on the integral role interactive technology has played in their lives. However, this is too simplistic and essentially deduces that (1) Gen Y has grown up playing interactive, technology-based games, (2) they like games, so (3) turning learning into games is the answer to training for Gen Y. Simulation and game mechanics have their place and certainly have efficacy as enhanced tools to develop skills in the workplace with Gen Y. So, gamification is likely here to stay. However, it should be considered only as a potential part of the overall equation and not a singular answer in the Millennial work-related learning environment.

3. Microlearning and Social Network Knowledge Sharing

Before delving into the theories of microlearning, it is important to understand their foundation in *"pull vs push"* training methodologies.

In most businesses today, despite the fact that employees require knowledge and learning in near real-time (i.e. while they are building the desk in our Ikea example), this is not how training is provided. The desk assembly example, when translated to the typical organization's current process would likely:

X Require the employee to be scheduled in a classroom training session on desk assembly, most probably a week or two in the future

X Involve the employee searching through a disorderly search engine within an internal knowledge base

X Result in the employee navigating an online library of self-paced, virtual training on desk assembly to locate a (hopefully) relevant module

X Prompt the employee to scan through their email archives to locate the link to a recorded webinar on desk assembly that they recall being distributed a few months back.

The previous two generations grew up in a time when physical storehouses of knowledge were required. Most Boomers and Gen Xers will recall utilizing the university library as the primary source for information and research. Now, the library is obsolete. Gen Y has grown up with immediate access to virtual storehouses of universal knowledge literally at their fingertips. When a trip to the library to access information was required, direct training where information was "*pushed*" to a learner was a useful way to integrate and thereby augment knowledge. This is not a necessity today given the exponential growth of communication technology over the past three decades. Information can now be "*pulled*" instantly and from anywhere.

Despite widespread disintermediation in the delivery channels of knowledge distribution, advances in technology have not been fully leveraged by business to create comprehensive "*pull*" learning. Corporations and training departments continue to produce "*push*" material. However, the formidable computational platforms, combined with Gen Y demand for real-time, on demand learning will lead to a new transformational paradigm in learning that will soon fully embrace "*pull*" methodologies.

"*Pull*" learning manifests in a state where learners assimilate material as opposed to materials being predetermined and presented. In essence, learning moves from a structured and programmed procedural activity to an on-demand organic dynamic.

When adding up the costs to develop and deliver traditional training, it befits today's corporations to invest in *"pull"* learning. By speeding up the transfer of knowledge, organizations can realize enormous bottom-line financial savings while simultaneously ensuring a Millennial-ready learning environment.

Once a strategy of *"pull vs push"* learning is adopted, the next critical milestone for any corporation is the development of microlearning. Microlearning is technology-based education that is short, delivered *just-in-time* and ideally embedded within a product, employee workflow application or an easy to access platform. Simplicity is the key. The goal is to impart required knowledge at the point of need in a short burst of relevant material. Microlearning requires that the knowledge is delivered immediately upon connecting to the learner and the transfer of knowledge is completed in ninety seconds. Why ninety seconds? There is ample research that suggests Gen Y (and most adults who utilize technology today) have an attention span that cannot exceed a minute and a half of intake without losing focus. If it takes longer than ninety seconds, **Leaky Knowledge** begins to occur.

Microlearning enhances **Maximized Assimilation of Knowledge** in the following ways:

- It is efficient in that it accounts for the 70:20:10 rule and does not invest considerable time in overly extensive, unilateral knowledge delivery that only results in 10% retention as most current training does.

- It delivers knowledge at 'the moment of impact' when the employee/learner requires it, to enhance their ability and skills in order to perform their job functions effectively.

- It adjusts for the attention span of adult learners and in doing so makes the best use of technology-based delivery in clear, relevant and quick techniques which leads to productivity.

- It leverages available technologies to create rich media, interactive and versatile experiences for learners without today's disproportionate investment in educational design.

As microlearning constructs are adopted in business and ultimately supplant traditional learning models, it is imperative to ensure that the delivery of content remains adaptive to individual learning styles. As previously outlined, training and learning for Gen Y will require increased focus on adaptation to individual learning styles. In the on-demand world of microlearning, the learning content needs to be developed to include all four styles. For example, a specific microlearning module might contemplate one-click video for the visual learner, a podcast format for the auditory learner, a demo or gamification-based play session for the kinesthetic and online Wikipedia-style content for the read/write learner.

Similar to how microlearning utilizes advancements in technology, social media and social networks can greatly enhance the learning experience through the exchange of knowledge. Social learning is the ability to connect and freely share ideas on what works and to be able to connect with others who are in the learning space. Learning and support from peers along with testing ideas and knowledge against peer input is critical. Gen Y has been connecting with this form of learning since they powered up their first laptop.

Learning for generations prior to Gen Y was some form of teacher-to-pupil articulation of information. As connectedness has proliferated in the past few decades, Gen Y has taken the peer and social learning concept to a new level. They want and need to immediately connect with others that are going through the same learning or requiring the same knowledge within their job function. They want to test and challenge new ideas not just with a trainer, teacher, manager or coach, but also with their peers. This leads to the requirement for companies to invest part of their learning efforts into informal platforms to encourage employee social connection in order to further advance *Maximized Assimilation of Knowledge.*

A 2015 study published by Microsoft actually determined that in digital social learning situations;

"...bursts of attention allow heavier users of social media to process information and encode it to memory more efficiently."

'Attention Spans'
Consumer Insights, Microsoft Canada
Spring, 2015

This is unquestionably food for thought for those business leaders still clinging to the idea that traditional classroom training is the most effective path to a knowledgeable workforce.

Colleges and universities have actually outpaced the business world in terms of adapting and progressing in these areas. The explosion of course material available in multiple formats with concise but abbreviated modules and content "bytes" has been molded to suit the requirements of Gen Y students. In many online college course formats, for instance, students pull content in prompt, short units according to their learning style; content is interactive; they participate in discussion boards and have access to professors or teaching assistants in real-time social applications. Corporations may want to look at these models to advance their learning programs toward microlearning and Social Knowledge-Sharing.

An example using our fictional characters will help to further frame these critical concepts.

—————————————————

Michelle is in James' office for her monthly review of her division's results. She is expressing her frustration at the fact that productivity is lagging behind budget and James is questioning how they could be behind when he approved five new hires in the previous quarter.

Michelle replies, "Yes, James, we got those new supply chain managers hired in record time. We've usually hired one at a time so I've never really had the same insight into how we transition new hires into the team as I have with hiring this big wave. It's pretty concerning, to be honest."

"What's the issue?" James responds.

Michelle explains that the new hires came out of the standard departmental two-month training class almost a month ago. She expected them to be prepared to start working with their suppliers, vendors and fulfilment partners on day one.

"I don't know what they did for eight weeks in that training room but they were not job-ready by any stretch of the imagination," she explains. "Now they are not contributing at the level I need them to meet our numbers. They are a drain on the rest of the team

as their peers try to bring them up to speed. And whose neck is on the line for the end results? Not the training department; it's mine!"

James contemplates the feedback for a minute. He recently completed a 2-hour online product training. The training was mandatory for all employees and was designed to introduce the company's workforce to new enhancements on their main product line. It was a self-paced training module that went through 40 slides and contained a few short quizzes interspersed between them to test the employee's comprehension of the new product features. About 30 minutes into the training, James had to admit he was pretty bored and he skipped quickly through the rest of the material: the quiz questions at the end weren't exactly challenging. After he completed it, he wanted to check in with some of his front-line employees to see what they thought of the new enhancements. With all the young employees on the team, he wondered if the training really resonated with them. The feedback that he received lit a lightbulb for him. The team all understood what the new product features were, but they really had no idea how they were going to incorporate them into their day-to-day jobs. One of the newer employees said that she would have preferred to play with the new software for a few days on her breaks to figure out how the features worked. Then at that point she would have been able to help her peers apply it.

"I think we need to look at an overhaul of our training practices across the board," James comments, "we've been doing things the same way for too long and what might have worked years ago just isn't cutting it for our people anymore."

Michelle decides to connect again with Tyler who has, in many ways, become a sounding board and great source of brainstorming within the team. She asks him to lead a "think tank" with a small group of employees: a mix of recent hires and tenured individuals, tasked with coming up with their ideal learning strategy for new employees.

The team meets regularly for several weeks and presents their initial findings to Michelle. She asks them to present more formally to both James and herself the following week. She is pleased to be able to provide her department's ideas in response to his stated desire for an overhaul of current training methodologies.

The team presents a model that is distinctly juxtaposed to current training programs and methods. It recommends that new hires begin with a short one-day introduction to the company and their specific division, delivered in a classroom format. Subsequently, they are assigned a mentor with whom to work for several days in order to get a sense of workflow and prioritization. The team suggests that technical training, which is self-paced and online, be shortened into much shorter segments. This is followed immediately by several days where the new employees actually do the activities just learned. It is recommended they have access to an online mentor with whom they can live chat if they have any immediate questions or need guidance. Further, they present how an internal social site, one in which employees can connect and both ask and respond to day-to-day questions will help all employees – especially new ones – efficiently gain knowledge on "how to" questions. Also recommended is that managers spend at least five to seven hours per week working with their new employees and providing input and direction.

James concludes the meeting by thanking Michelle, Tyler and the team. He feels they are on the right path. Next, he wants to explore the options presented with a broader group of senior leaders to see how they can be refined into a revised new-employee transition process.

In summary, learning and training within corporations is in dire need of a transformational shift. Current approaches are outdated and require massive investment that often cannot be shown to have tangible returns. As Gen Y increasingly embeds in the workplace, comprehensive learning strategies which encompass the principles of dominant learning styles and move to on the job, coaching-based foundations, will succeed. In addition, online training and self-paced learning need to be revamped to be more interactive and succinct, and technology should be leveraged more deeply to create connections where employees can learn from peers.

6.

"I know everyone thinks people in my age group want to be President before we are 30. The truth is - I'd rather have some balance, a great boss and a fun place to work at. Sure, I want to advance and I want to make money. Who doesn't? But learning more, contributing more and being appreciated for what I do is my main motivation."

29 year-old employee
in a large corporation
Generation Y

Career Development: Forward vs Upward

When you really dig in to what Millennials seek in terms of their own career development, you find that it is a matter of *Forward vs Upward.*

Boomers and Gen X have a much greater predilection for climbing the corporate ladder than their Gen Y counterparts. Gen Ys do want to progress and a contingent have their eye on the C-level, but Millennials tend to seek knowledge, increased accountability and variety. They want career growth, but it is not always in the form of climbing another upward rung on the metaphorical ladder. They want to contribute and feel that their work has real meaning.

In an August 2009 *Harvard Business Publishing* interview Sylvia Ann Hewlett, president of the Center for Work-Life Policy referred to a Gen Y desire for development as having an "Odyssey" principle. Hewlett explains that Millennials value and are incentivized by non-financial or hierarchical position-related growth opportunities. According to her, Gen Ys "*crave a range of new experiences...such as a global assignment...*" or other opportunities outside their day-to-day functions that serve to enrich their knowledge and involvement in the overall business.

Leaders, along with their Human Resources support teams, need to be deliberate in designing newly systematized approaches to employee development. There are three fundamental areas that are critical for business leaders and HR professionals to address:

1. Mentoring
2. Team-based Stretch Assignments
3. Learning for Self-Development

1. Mentoring

Mentoring in the business context is generally defined as a relationship under which a more experienced or skilled employee provides advice and counseling to a more junior or less experienced employee.

From a business leader's point of view, the most important step in implementing an effective mentoring initiative involves collaborating from step one with HR. Human Resources can provide significant support to business leaders by developing and implementing well-defined and formalized mentoring initiatives. In most instances, this will entail the pairing of a more junior, presumably Gen Y, employee with a higher-level manager or leader within the organization. Effective mentoring programs maintain a firm schedule with mentor and mentee meeting at regular intervals. The meetings should be kept confidential and subject matter unrestricted. While this guide is focused on the relevant elements of Gen Y mentoring, it should be noted that mentoring programs should not be limited strictly to junior employees. Mentorships can be fluid and match specific employee needs at specific times in their career; they do not have to be permanent.

In many instances, beyond providing advice for specific workplace items, mentors will recommend reading materials and introduce their mentee employees to other influential leaders in the organization. As much as possible, a leader mentoring a Gen Y employee has an opportunity to focus heavily and demonstrate a vested interest in their career development while helping to break down internal barriers to support the employee. In addition, when mentoring a Gen Y employee, it is important to avoid a myopic perspective that focuses exclusively on the internal company. It is important to encourage Gen Y employees to utilize the technologies that come naturally in order to further expand their individual professional networks.

For a Gen Y employee, mentoring has a variety of benefits directly related to their career development. These include:

- Building a network they can draw from, in order to build opportunities for increased knowledge.

- Receiving feedback which can directly assist in learning to navigate both the internal and external business environments.

- Obtaining guidance and support related to the seeking out of new development opportunities.

For organizations, the benefits of establishing a HR-supported and administered mentoring program include the following:

- Employee retention, particularly with Gen Y employees who may not know how to begin the development process. Mentoring actively manages their development.

- From an organizational planning perspective, mentoring provides an excellent basis for identification and development of key talent.

- Driving additional productivity as stretch assignments and knowledge growth opportunities are isolated and acted upon.

The role of HR in developing a mentoring initiative is highlighted because it is essential that these programs are managed effectively. Often, if they are less formally administrated, they tend to lose momentum and the net benefits add diminishing returns over time. HR's function in establishing a mentoring construct is expansive and intensive, it includes:

- ✓ Developing the program and defining business rules and standards for participation.
- ✓ Appropriately matching employees and leaders.
- ✓ Marketing the program.
- ✓ Continuous evaluation and oversight.

For the business leader embarking on a mentoring relationship, The Center For Mentoring Excellence outlines ten best practices for the mentor as follows:

Start by getting to know your mentee
Make sure you take time to get to know your mentee before you jump into the work of mentoring. Nothing of substance will happen until you establish a trusting relationship.

Establish working agreements
Agreements lay the foundation of a mentoring relationship. Build in basic structures about how you will work together moving forward. Make sure you and your mentee agree on ground rules.

Focus on developing robust learning goals
The purpose of mentoring is to learn. Learning is also the payoff. Make sure the mentee's learning goals are worthy of your time and effort. Developing robust learning goals takes time and good conversation.

Balance talking and listening
It's easy and natural to want to give advice, especially because you've "been there and done that." But mentees want more than good advice. They want you to listen to their ideas as much as they want to hear what you have to say.

Ask questions rather than give answers
Take the time to draw out a mentee's thinking and get them to reflect on their own experience. Ask probing questions that encourage them to come up with their own insights.

Engage in meaningful and authentic conversation

Strive to go deeper than surface conversation. Share your own successes and failures as well as what you are learning from your current mentoring relationship.

Check out assumptions and hunches

If you sense something is missing or not going well, you are probably right. Address issues as soon as possible. Simply stating, "I want to check out my assumption which is ..." will prevent you from assuming your mentee is on track.

Support and challenge your mentee

Work on creating a comfortable relationship first before you launch into the uncomfortable stretch needed for deep learning. Mentees need to feel supported (comfortable) and yet be challenged (a little uncomfortable) in order to grow and develop.

Set the expectation of two-way feedback

Candid feedback is a powerful trigger for growth and change. Set the expectation early on. Be prepared to offer candid feedback, balanced with compassion. Model how to ask for and receive good feedback by asking your mentee for specific feedback on your own mentoring contribution.

Check in regularly to stay on track

Keep connected and develop a pattern of regular engagement. Both partners need to be accountable for following through with agreements. By holding an open, honest conversation about how you're doing and what you need to do to improve, you encourage mutual accountability and deepen the relationship.

"Top 10 Best Practices For Mentors"
www.centerformentoringexcellence.com
April 28, 2015

2. Team-based Stretch Assignments

It has been well established that Millennials want to work in team-based environments and often value the group over the individual. This team orientation stems from a deeply embedded propensity to share knowledge and coordinate with others who bring diverse skills to a team setting. This is also in stark contrast to the Boomer and Gen X collective character which is heavily individualized.

If we examine this tendency to gravitate to team-oriented activities alongside the fact that Gen Y desires knowledge-broadening experiences as part of their career development, a self-evident solution presents itself. By providing stretch assignments (i.e. assigned initiatives or projects outside of core accountabilities) and by configuring these in a team-based approach, ideal Gen Y career development opportunities are produced. In addition, given the available and preferential norm of distributed technology within a company, these can and often should constitute virtual teams. Virtual teamwork is a critical adaptation in today's business environment as it leverages the ability to create teams with complimentary skill sets without geographical restriction. This, in turn, drives improved productivity.

Despite the utilization of the wide variety of technology available to support virtual teamwork, many of today's predominantly Boomer and Gen X leaders have not fully embraced it. There is some lingering reticence regarding moving away from the face-to-face environment when forming teams. There is typically some level of usage of live chat, collaborative webinars, project management collaboration sites, and/or desktop video conferencing. Yet, despite the availability of this broad assortment of technologies that facilitate virtual teamwork, their utilization and adoption have not been wholly espoused. This leads to frustration in Gen Y who is eager to utilize all the available tools and network with a wide variety of their peers. The virtual team workspace can be tapped into as a source to foster community and connect teams to their shared purpose – this is, in fact, a must when developing teams whose constituents are from the Gen Y cohort.

In terms of the composition of the specific team stretch assignment itself, it is recommended that the following key guidelines be followed:

Make it **relevant** - an initiative that connects the team to the overall strategic objectives of the company, division or business unit.

"Millennials worry about teamwork and having meaningful work, [so] to attract the top [talent] it is important to demonstrate the value of work and the opportunity to build community with your team."

Lisa Ritchie, Match Marketing Group
"4 Critical Mistakes to Avoid When Hiring Gen Y"
Nicole Fallon
Business News Daily
October 28, 2014

Make it **challenging** – ensure it is not a "cakewalk" to achieve but a real business problem that needs to be solved; Gen Y wants to be tested.

"Gen Y welcome the opportunity to challenge outdated ways of working that are entrenched in the organisational culture. They love to be incentivised to work with employers, to reshape job roles so that they are more effective and bring that crucial work-life balance. Organisations need to ensure there are opportunities to voice ideas, plans and concerns."

"What Do Generation Y Really Want?"
Carina Paine Schofield, Ashridge Business School
HRZone
www.hrzone.com
July 9, 2014

Make it **diverse** – bring employees from different roles, levels and backgrounds; Gen Y values and intuitively harness the effectiveness of diverse teams.

141 ~ R U READY 4 Y?

"Diversity has been demonstrated to be a desirable and healthy workplace component. Generation Y members are open-minded and accepting of those different from themselves. Working and interacting with people outside of their own ethnic group is the norm. Not only are Gen Yers comfortable with the increasingly diverse workforce and client base, but also make others feel comfortable, which greatly benefits organizations."

"Understanding Generation Y"
White Paper – with Buddy Hobart, Solutions 21
© PrincetonOne
www.PrincetonOne.com
7/31/2008

Make it **fun** – encourage the team to name their project, define key success factors and milestones in advance and celebrate these as a group.

"Managers know and research (Sheahan, 2005) has demonstrated that happiness directly relates to productivity; to keep the best employees, managers must keep them happy which means making the Generation Y employee work environment fun. As the CEO of Zappos stated, creating a fun culture for employees boosts productivity and employee retention."

"Seven Tips for Managing Generation Y"
Kilber/Barclay/Ohmer – Northern State University
Journal of Management Policy and Practice Vol/15(4)
2014.

3. Learning for Self-Development

Not only are Millennials the most educated generation to hit the workforce, they show no inclination toward concluding their education after launching their careers.

The Yahoo Jobs survey previously referenced in Chapter 3 found that of the Gen Ys surveyed…

"….73 percent, nearly three out of four of those surveyed say it is likely they'll go back to school to obtain another academic degree/certification."
Generation Y: What Millennial Works Want: How To Attract and
Retain Gen Y Employees.
Yahoo Hotjobs/Robert Half International
2007

This further substantiates the ***Forward vs Upward*** principle. Millennials do not seek additional educational experiences as a means to continuously add credentials for bigger and better paying positions; whereas, this is precisely the dynamic that is prevalent in the Boomer and Gen X mindset. Gen Y seeks these as opportunities to expand their knowledge and grow. This represents a huge opportunity for businesses that recognize and act on Gen Y's desire to augment their education. How can they do this? There are two main strategies that leaders and HR professionals should endorse and execute:

1. Internal – Learning Integration with Talent Management Systems

Most large organizations have some form of Talent Management System that assimilates performance goals and objectives with globally standardized applications for evaluation and feedback. Smaller organizations often have a Talent Management process if a specific software solution is not utilized. Integrating educational offerings and tracking into a Talent Management framework (ideally in a digital application), accommodates the technology-focused and connected working expectations of Gen Y. Gen Y's thirst for knowledge and education can be satisfied by training where they can build an internal profile of learning experience that ties directly to their performance feedback and assessment. Essentially, employees are able to create a self-directed informal certification in areas of education that pertain directly to the company itself and their role or future role in it.

2. External – Education Support, Tuition Reimbursement and Investing in Education

Many companies have offered tuition reimbursement programs for their employees in the past. This benefit has increased in the past several decades and it will be a necessity with Gen Y.

Tuition reimbursement programs can be directed specifically at job-related development courses and degrees, or can be more open-ended in terms of subject areas being studied. In addition, some companies require that employees make a commitment to remain for a prescribed period after completion of a company-funded degree or program. This practice has been questioned in terms of its efficacy as it is derived from a fear that employees will use a new educational milestone to find a job outside the organization. This will be a challenge with Gen Y who value trust and look for this in their employer. In the end, the more open and unrestricted a tuition reimbursement program is, the more it will resonate with Gen Y.

As Luke Landes elaborates:

"Only the companies without confidence in its own ability to attract qualified employees need to handcuff its employees who seek additional education — generally a more ambitious group than average — to the company for several years."

"Tuition Reimbursement: A Benefit for Some
Employees and Employers"
Luke Landes
Forbes/Consumerism Commentary
July 16, 2012

Tuition reimbursement does not need to entail 100% coverage. In most instances, companies pay a portion of tuition or have an annual cap or threshold for reimbursement. In addition, these often require a certain grade to be attained and the courses to be completed in a specified period which fosters return on investment for the program.

If tuition reimbursement is not viable within certain business settings, there are other ways to invest by bringing education to employees. Many educational institutes and private training companies will provide standard courses, degrees and certifications or customize programs for companies. For Gen Ys, this is less ideal than tuition reimbursement as it does not provide the same flexibility to chart their own educational path. However, it is a viable alternative investment in education that will, at a minimum, provide opportunity for the Gen Y employee to participate in continuing education. In summary, leaders of Gen Y work environments need to develop a comprehensive strategic approach to career development that embraces the *Forward vs Upward* approach and incorporates the key elements of mentoring, team-based stretch assignment opportunities and education.

7.

"Once we started working together to figure out our own schedules, everyone stopped complaining and we actually starting getting things done for our customers. And our results show how effective taking control for ourselves has been."

Employee participant
in self-managed team
Gen Y

All Roads Lead to Team Self-Management

Team self-management may sound like a foreign concept to most Boomer and Gen X business leaders. Most are familiar with traditionally hierarchical management structures. For the majority, matrix organizations represent the deepest a business is willing to extend in terms of what is considered "leading edge".

As we look to the long-term, there is a pressing need to consider not only the fact that attitudes of the workforce are transforming as a result of the growing Gen Y domination, but business conditions themselves are increasing in complexity which further drives the need for changes. This calls for thinking that transcends the traditional organizational structures of (1) functional, (2) divisional, and (3) matrix.

Dissecting the insights provided in the preceding chapters, a narrative begins to emerge that clearly speaks to the key concepts of teamwork and flexibility. It is a narrative to which today's business leaders should pay close attention. All indications point toward team self-management as being the point where the essential Gen Y work environment begins to manifest itself. Teams and more to the point, deployment of discreet, sometimes impermanent and highly autonomous teams are where current leadership attention needs to be.

The concept of teams is critical to the future of business. Author of *Doing More With Teams: The New Way to Winning*, Bruce Piasecki explains;

"The magic I explore is what happens when individuals cohere in teams. Teams exceed the capabilities of exceptional individuals. Even a great individual is a composite of many people helping them compete."

"Effective Team Building Is The New Way To Win."

Rebecca Shafer

Business Insider

February 7, 2014

The businesses of the future that will boast the most successful management structures will have vertical, horizontal, oblique and intersecting flows of skills, accountabilities and information. Obviously, this becomes more difficult to control and manage as the group of employees becomes larger. Small, focused teams which come together for either a specific short-term purpose or a medium/longer-term operational requirement represent the most proficient means of managing. Ironically, they also represent the work environments that will result most profoundly in Gen Y productivity and engagement.

While the concept of team self-management resonates with some of today's leaders, businesses have been slow to unequivocally commit to and execute on the idea. Those who are acutely aware of the innovations that will be required as Gen Ys influence continues have started to adopt it.

Chuck Blakeman, writer, TEDx speaker and founder of Crankset Group attributes much of this slow adoption to a tendency to cling to the paradigms and practices of the traditional Industrial Age. Blakeman argues convincingly that these old school ideas and benchmarks are in conflict with what he describes as the Participation Age, where the meaning of work and collective membership in an organization's vision and growth are paramount. The Participation Age that Blakeman delineates lines up seamlessly with the requirements of Gen Y:

"The hallmarks of the Participation Age are simple, participation and sharing. Companies are discovering that if they invite everyone to participate in the building of a great company, and to share in the rewards, both the company and the people, profit more. The Participation Age is also creating workplaces with a soul. This isn't woo-woo crap; these are hard-core success strategies. And it isn't a fringe idea. Those who embrace the Participation Age will thrive; those who don't will be left behind."

"Embracing the Participation Age".
Chuck Blakeman
www.inc.com
July 15, 2014

One has to wonder about the reticence to move more closely to team self-management, especially since it works! Going back as far as 2005 and extending to 2011, QSM conducted an extensive study of schedule compression in the software development process. The results strongly supported the concept of small, focused teams delivering the highest quality and productivity. By combining the small team with structure that reduced the level of detailed management oversight, the results were even more dramatic. Analyzing over three decades of data, the study found that:

"A key characteristic of these top performing projects was the use of small teams... larger teams realized modest schedule compression on small projects, but saw little or no improvement in time to market for larger

projects. Regardless of project size, the large team strategy drastically increased cost and reduced quality."

"Small Teams Deliver Lower Cost, Higher Quality."

Kate Armel

www.qsm.com

January 26, 2012

A considerable amount of accountability for business not embracing team self-management lies with leadership and management themselves. Breaking away from the conventional edicts that stress and reinforce controls as the overriding role of managers is problematic for many. This was a factor discussed in Chapter 2 around flexibility with work schedules and locations as well. With team self-management, the focus of front-line management shifts from managing metrics and implementing multi-layered control configurations to focusing on the deliverables and goals to be achieved within business units, team facilitation and initiatives. The fluidity required within the organization's operations makes a number of Boomer and Gen X leaders hesitant as this fluidity is inherently more ambiguous.

"The major obstacle to self-management, as one might suspect, was thought to be people, especially managers. C. J. Cullinane identified the most important requirement for self-management success as 'conviction and commitment of top management.'"

"Are We Ready for Self-Management?"

James Hesket

Harvard Business School – HBS Working Knowledge

September 1, 2006

As described in the content of this guide, Gen Y gravitates to work conditions that enable them to make more decisions, predominantly within teams and environments that enable them to experiment with ideas as they work to achieve objectives. Overcoming innate resistance and the resulting inertia, and moving to team self-management models simply make sense for leaders preparing for Millennial domination in their ranks.

The good news is that Gen Y is well-equipped to assume greater accountability for decision-making and undertaking solutions that will accomplish business goals through their participation in working teams. These capabilities exceed those that Gen X employees exhibited at the same point in their careers. Millennials are significantly more advanced in the following core competencies:

Influence:

- Gen Y understands the decision-making processes and has grown up in team-based environments. This experience has provided them with the ability to effectively state their case and make compelling cases for their points of view.

Adaptability:

- Gen Y is the first generation to experience the degree and rapidity of change that technology advancement has introduced. They are accustomed to and comfortable with constant variation and adjust to it with greater ease than any of their predecessor generations.

Service-Orientation:

- Gen Ys inherently understand the value of quality service for today's businesses. When tackling business challenges, Millennials intrinsically develop solutions and ideas that contribute to the bottom-line, while keeping customer needs the centralizing tenet within the business equation.

Collaboration:

- Gen Y is all about the social elements of work. This means an appetite for open interchange and communication. They have a strong conviction that engaging within a team setting represents the most expeditious way to resolve business issues.

Results-Orientation:

- Implementing innovative and sustainable methods to achieve desired results is a core proficiency of Gen Y. This makes them apposite for self-guidance and team self-regulation mechanisms given that the collective goal of the team always remains in sight.

Rolling out a team self-management approach is well-suited to the soon-to-be incumbent employee base within corporations. Further underpinning the rationale for implementing this type of structure is a well-known and time-tested property of industrial psychology: the Hawthorne Effect.

The Hawthorne Studies, conducted in the 1920s, frequently refer to the illumination studies they were intended to evaluate and only occasionally mention other key findings from the project. These related directly to the social impacts on productivity behavior within working teams.

The studies involved measuring the productivity of a telephone relay assembly operation. Subjects were ostensibly being tested on the impacts of illumination or lighting alterations on efficiency. At its core, the study concluded that there is a form of reactivity which boosts productivity when employees are aware they are being studied. More relevant, however, were the notable findings around the effects on output when a group has an objective and works as a team to achieve these objectives.

Employees who were part of the study operated under a variety of changing conditions and the introduction of a mix of challenges. In all instances, they were able to overcome these changes and challenges as a cohesive group and deliver beyond productivity goals. When interviewed, the participants attributed their success to:

- ✓ Team co-operation and engagement.
- ✓ Coordination of individual skills and work preferences.
- ✓ Freedom to work and complete functions without constant oversight.
- ✓ The sense that they were part of something special.

The Hawthorne Effect and, in particular, the telephone relay assembly project teams, further substantiate the effectiveness of breaking business operations into small, focused and self-managed teams. The Hawthorne Studies made it clear that the social impact of peer groups can have more influence than management control and decision-making. Again, this known social-psychological fact can be readily harnessed within the Gen Y workforce; a workforce that values flexibility, team collaboration and innovation toward a common goal.

There are many examples within leading organizations, such as Google's "dog food teams", predicated on the notion of teams of employees using its beta applications and driving product improvement. This is a type of bottom-up solution-orientation that facilities team-based productivity without a lot of bureaucratic rules or micro-controlled management oversight.

Moving to team self-management is unavoidable when readying business for Gen Y and the benefits are far-reaching and include:

Benefit One – Team Self-Management Fosters Flexibility and Speed

- Elimination of unnecessary bureaucracy, departmental control and top-down management.

- Practices and processes can be expeditiously adapted to fluctuating circumstances, eliminating the inefficiencies of tight processes, hierarchical decision-making and restrictive controls.

Benefit Two – Team Self-Management Builds in Cost-Efficiency

- Cost-savings achieved through the fewer levels of management required and increasing the span of control for existing managers.

- Advancing solutions to business problems evolves to an organic process that does not require additional investment.

Benefit Three - Team Self-Management Facilitates Effective Customer Service

- At the end of the day, businesses are in business to gain and retain customers and work effectively with partners. Team self-management empowers employee teams to meet customer needs expediently and, consequently, making customer experience increasingly effortless.

- Employees learn to act independently and draw on the team's expertise, which increases knowledge and enables higher quality and faster solutions to customer challenges.

Benefit Four - Self-Managed Teams Require Less Investment in Policy-making and Business Rule Development

- As team members understand each other's unique capabilities, contributions and expertise, they work together to meet the expected results and develop their own unique standards and work practices.

- This facilitates voluntary compliance to business requirements more suitably than management personnel having to enforce this; team members provide the peer pressure for each individual to perform to the required standards, as under-performance is addressed within the team.

Benefit Five – Team Self-Management Evolves the Role of Manager

- Managers advance to the role of facilitators, coaches and mentors which further enables the progression of employee learning, recognition and development.

- Managers lead from a goal-oriented perspective and invest time in people and results-based initiatives, leading to attainment of business results.

Another revolutionary thought springs from the team self-management theory: job sharing. The concept of employees contributing to multiple interrelated job functions is one that has not been extensively promoted within corporations. True team self-management leads to this type of situation naturally and; again, fits ideally with the needs, wants and expectations of Gen Y. Imagine a scenario where an employee moves from function-to-function based on real-time business drivers, such as customer need, supply, work volumes or as part of a designed process to address resource scarcity or fill downtime. The potential efficiencies that can be realized are limitless and not out of reach for most businesses with the right investments in technology.

Case Study in Team Self-Management:

For those who still believe that self-managed teams will only lead to chaos and confusion, outlined below is a real example where a team self-management model was adopted with a team of Gen Y employees and led to significant results. This was conducted as a pilot and the authors recently had the opportunity to interview the executive responsible for the business unit.

Company: *Large Consulting and Business Process Outsourcing Firm*

Operation: *Client Call Center*

Location: *Toronto, Canada*

Business Problem: *Customers with multiple products from the same company were expressing dissatisfaction with mean time to resolve service inquiries and having to contact individual departments themselves to track and report progress.*

Goals of the Pilot: *Offer customers one team that could service all of their products.*

Constraints: *Solution could not add to cost or management overhead.*

Approach:
- *A team, later named the All-In-One Support Center, consisting of five core employees was selected (geographically dispersed in four Canadian provinces):*

  a. *Three employees skilled in Product A (due to this being the bulk of the queries/ requests)*
  b. *One employee skilled in Product B*
  c. *One employee skilled in Product C*

- *A select set of several hundred customers who required frequent and specialized services, identified as high volume users of the call centers, were assigned to the team.*

- *The team consisted exclusively of Gen Y employees who were informed they would be self-managed; a manager from an adjunct department would assist with any coordination or high-level direction but would not be involved in the day-to-day.*

- *The All-In-One team was provided laptops and the required technology. Live chat, email and a toll-free number were provided to the customers as contact points for support.*

- *The team was instructed they could set their own schedules and work both at the office, or remotely, but were encouraged to have a balanced mix as face-to-face time was considered important. They needed to ensure they would always have coverage to support customers on a twelve-hour per business day basis.*

- *It was expected that the team members would meet and come up with a plan to support and cross-train each other over time as opposed to providing formal training.*

- *The team was not provided any specific metrics; such as speed of answer, time to resolve issue or email response times. Instead they were to be measured on two metrics only: i) customer retention for their assigned base; ii) customer satisfaction based on surveys that were conducted every three months.*

- *The team was encouraged to meet regularly to share ideas on how to better service the customer base; to implement and experiment with those ideas, and to focus, as much as possible, on being proactive.*

Results:

- *The **business results** were astounding:*

  - ✓ *10% increase in customer retention of 400 basis points over the first year.*
  - ✓ *300% reduction in call volumes.*
  - ✓ *80% adoption of live chat as a service channel for customers.*
  - ✓ *Issue resolution improved from an average of 4 days to less than 24 hours.*
  - ✓ *Customer satisfaction rates consistently above 95% which represented an increase of more than 15% based on historical data.*

- *The **employee results** were equally impressive:*

  - ✓ *Employee engagement scores for the All-In-One team were significantly higher than the corporate or divisional average.*
  - ✓ *The All-In-One team became an incubator for new service innovations that were later adopted for the broader business unit.*
  - ✓ *All-In-One team members were highly recognized and experienced a 100% employee retention status for over 18-months after the original launch.*
  - ✓ *After two years, the team's success was so great that the call center was deconstructed and the five-employee team with an assigned customer base model was rolled out across the business with similar positive results.*

✓ *Managers actually became significantly more involved in motivating and coaching employees rather than focusing on daily metrics.*

The above example can be used by business leaders in consideration of adapting a similar pilot or expanded structure.

As drastic and different team self-management seems, it is the strong contention of the authors that it is a cornerstone to the overall success of future execution in business with Gen Y employees. While it typically meets with skepticism from seasoned Gen X or even Boomer leaders (usually with a plethora of reasons why "it won't work" in their unique companies) it marries impeccably with the equally transformative Gen Y outlook on their careers. And, it can and will bring out the best in the Millennial workforce which has abundant talent to supply. The corporations and leaders of corporations that understand this, and understand it early, will win.

8.

"Once we embraced the value of the generational differences and realized that Gen Y was fundamentally different, but extremely adept, we started making some major changes and saw progress beyond what we had imagined."

59 year-old
corporate executive
Baby Boomer

T.T.Y.L.

Before rushing to Google to translate the textese above, it stands for "talk to you later". But first, let us quickly summarize several of the main themes and approaches to Gen Y that were covered in this guide.

The advancing wave of Millennials into the business employment pool is real and has real consequences. Despite the fact that some of the myths around Gen Y career mindsets are embellished or overblown, the changes that need to be made to adapt to their true expectations are both transformational and beneficial to the bottom-line. Boomers and Gen X who hold the majority of management and leadership positions in corporations today need to take accountability for implementing these changes effectively. To not act on this is detrimental to a business' future. Appropriately adapting and preparing will enable companies to leverage the highly-educated and highly-capable Gen Y employee base.

In order to accomplish this, today's business leaders must concentrate their strategies and subsequent efforts on redeveloping their approach to employee engagement. This can be accomplished by adopting the three key foundational areas of focus toward engagement: (1) Approach to Technology; (2) Innovation Focus and (3) Location and Schedule Flexibility. In addition, acknowledging the magnitude of the role recognition plays within the Gen Y cohort and taking action to build a recognition culture is essential. This includes a methodical and considered system of rewards that are meaningful to the Millennial employee population; investing in social recognition through peer-to-peer constructs and understanding that leadership, communication and feedback are also now key components of recognition. It is critical that business leaders practice Senior Management Connectedness (SMC) and remain visible, accessible, flexible and above all, maintain integrity.

Career development needs to take on more of a forward vs upward philosophy which supports a range of new experiences for Gen Y employees. Investing in comprehensive and ubiquitous mentoring within the organization is important.

Arranging for team-based stretch assignments that challenge employees and implementing a purposeful and well-structured strategy around education are fundamental to career development. Beyond this, reconstructing corporate training in a manner that moves away from conventional, outdated classroom-based methodologies, is necessary. Learning must go through a wholesale metamorphosis toward a Maximized Assimilation of Knowledge paradigm that is both comprehensive and does not rely exclusively or too heavily on the current trend of gamification.

Similarly, the corporate brand needs to be one that will resonate with Gen Y. While some companies have led in producing these types of brands, many more must focus their efforts here in order to ensure they can attract and retain Gen Y talent. The "how, where and when" of branding as it pertains to recruitment requires significant rethinking as well. And, finally, the corporate culture and brand should embrace social responsibility, diversity and inclusion.

All of the above provides a compelling line of reasons toward an organizational structure which contemplates deployment of small, self-managed teams. Team self-management represents a framework that addresses Millennials' employment and work expectations, is inherently efficient and comprises very few obstacles in implementing.

In summary, there is extensive benefit to be derived for organizations that welcome this new breed of employee into the corporate fold. The changes required are dramatic and all-encompassing. Those business leaders who develop a deep understanding of the key concepts offered in this guide and move to transform their companies to leverage Gen Y talent will undoubtedly thrive well into the future.

Author Profiles

LUBAINA GALELY

Lubaina has leveraged almost two decades of global experience in multiple continents with a focus on customer loyalty and project management leadership roles. Her impressive track record includes building and driving high-performance teams across multiple business lines and countries within the airline and retail industries and most recently with global HR BPO firms. In addition to her MBA and PMP, Lubaina holds over 11 designations and professional qualifications and has won numerous prestigious awards, including the CPA National and Ontario Gold Awards, LOMA Americas Top PCS and Top ACS Awards.

WHITNEY WRONA

Whitney began her 15-year career in the Heath Care Insurance and Benefits industry and has extensive experience in Human Capital Management with a focus on the fields of Training & Learning Management, Leadership Facilitation, Employee Engagement and Performance Consulting. Working across North America, Europe and Asia, she has been able to help drive a unified approach to service within a Fortune 500 organization. She holds Bachelor's degrees in Consumer Science and Speech Communication. In addition, Whitney is a Certified Master Facilitator with AchieveGlobal-MHIGlobal and holds a Certificate in Training from Yale University.

ANTHONY HORTON

Over the past 20 years, Anthony's career has included executive and senior leadership positions with Fortune 500 and global corporations in the Telecommunications, Business Process Outsourcing and Human Capital Management industries. He has a passion for innovation and creatively organizes diverse teams and work methodologies to foster employee engagement and customer loyalty. He holds Honors B.A. and Master's degrees from the University of Waterloo and an Advanced Certificate in Strategic Human Resource Management from Cornell University.

The authors would like to thank the outstanding companies, leaders, peers and colleagues who over the years have encouraged and inspired us to continuously learn, think and act.

Special appreciation also to Louise Paulson for her support and input and Harriett Thompson (@ harriets_world) for the professional photographs.

Printed in the United States
By Bookmasters